MARCO

Tips

FLORENCE

GERMANY

SWITZERLAND AUSTRIA

ITALY SLOVENIA

FRANCE Genoa CROATIA

MC Florence

RSM BOSNIA-
HERZEG.

Corsica
(F) Rome

Naples

Sardinia Ischia
(I)

*Mediterranean
Sea*

SYMBOLS

INSIDER TIP — Insider Tip
★ — Highlight
●●●● — Best of ...
☄ — Scenic view
☺ — Responsible travel: for
ecological or fair trade
aspects
(*) — Telephone numbers that
are not toll-free

PRICE CATEGORIES HOTELS

Expensive	over 170 euros
Moderate	100–170 euros
Budget	under 100 euros

Prices are for a double room
per night, breakfast usually
included

PRICE CATEGORIES RESTAURANTS

Expensive	over 30 euros
Moderate	15–30 euros
Budget	under 15 euros

Prices are for a typical complete meal

On the cover: Galleria dell'Accademia p. 41, Rivoire p. 62

CONTENTS

Shopping → p. 70

Entertainment → p. 80

Where to stay → p. 88

Street atlas → p. 120

DID YOU KNOW?
Courses → p. 20
City sightseeing → p. 22
City lights → p. 37
Sport-crazy → p. 39
Keep fit → p. 44
Relax & enjoy → p. 58
Local specialities → p. 64
Gourmet restaurants → p. 66
Made to measure → p. 77
Medici villas → p. 78
Books & films → p. 86
Luxury hotels → p. 92
Currency converter → p. 111

MAPS IN THE GUIDEBOOK
(122 A1) Page numbers and coordinates refer to the street atlas and the map of Florence and surrounding area on p. 132/133
(0) Site/address located off the map
Coordinates are also given for places that are not marked on the street atlas.
A plan of the public transport network can be found inside the back cover

INSIDE BACK COVER: PULL-OUT MAP →

PULL-OUT MAP 𝄞
(𝄞 A–B 2–3) Refers to the removable pull-out map

The best MARCO POLO Insider Tips

Our top 15 Insider Tips

BEST OF ...

FOR FREE

● *City tour with bus no. C3*
The *electric minibus* drives through the narrow streets of old Florence, past the Piazza Pitti and Piazza Santa Croce and crosses the Arno several times a day. This makes it the cheapest city tour – not completely free of course, but for a mere 1.20 euros → p. 112

● *A break at the library*
You can sit virtually undisturbed under the arcades of the cloisters at the *Biblioteca delle Oblate*. Brunelleschi's dome is so close you could almost touch it, and there's a play area for the kids. The setting costs nothing, so you can treat yourself to a cappuccino and a brioche (photo, below) → p. 50

● *Loggia dei Lanzi*
Perhaps the finest Florentine sculpture gallery stands out in the open, and there's not even an admission charge. Here, you are surrounded by works by great artists such as Giambologna, Michelangelo or Donatello → p. 33

● *Fiesole's fantastic view*
A steep path leads from the piazza in Fiesole up to the *San Francesco Monastery* and the highest point in the area. The view over the city and the Arno valley is breathtaking, admission – and thought – is free → p. 101

● *Cimitero degli Inglesi*
In the 19th century, Alfred Böcklin's Isle of the Dead was the last stop on many a Northern European's 'Grand Tour'. Non-Catholics, especially English, French or Russian by birth, lie buried here between the cypresses and roses. Take a stroll over the cemetery and enjoy its peacefulness, free of charge → p. 41

● *Fuochi di San Giovanni*
Since the 14th century, Florence has celebrated its patron saint on 24 June. To mark the occasion, the city puts on a fabulous *firework display* for its residents and guests below the Piazzale Michelangelo → p. 105

●●●● Dots in guidebook refer to 'Best of ...' tips

● *Ponte Vecchio*

The Old Bridge is at its most beautiful when the city lights reflected in the Arno compete with the sparkle of the jewellery in the tiny shops on the bridge (photo, right) → p. 39

● *Uffizi*

Offices *(uffizi)* to accommodate the regional administration: that was Vasari's original brief when Cosimo I commissioned the building in 1559. Today, the *Galleria degli Uffizi* is famous the world over → p. 32

● *Florentine bargains*

Years ago, the Florentine hats were sold at the *Mercato San Lorenzo.* Nowadays it's not so easy finding a typical Tuscan souvenir, but it's fun trying as you stroll around the market → p. 77

● *Sweeten your day*

The *Café Rivoire* has always been a good place to immerse yourself in Florentine life. Come here to see and be seen – and drink the best hot chocolate in town → p. 62

● *Gelato artigianale*

From simple dealer in dairy produce to world-famous ice cream parlour: Despite stiff competition, *Vivoli* is still the Florentine ice cream parlour par excellence! The ice cream is made to traditional recipes and is exported on special occasions from the heart of Florence even as far as Australia → p. 63

● *Medieval luxury*

Do you fancy seeing how the rich families of 13th-century Florence lived? Just visit the *Museo dell'Antica Casa Fiorentina* in the Palazzo Davanzati. You'll be surprised at the degree of comfort which existed even then → p. 36

● *Scale Brunelleschi's dome*

It is 116.5 m in height and still dominates the city skyline. If you can talk yourself into tackling the arduous climb up to the *dome*, you will be richly rewarded with the chance to see the 16th-century frescos close up → p. 30

ONLY IN

BEST OF ...

AND IF IT RAINS?
Activities to brighten your day

● **Museo Nazionale del Bargello**
Italy's most famous sculpture gallery is housed in the former city prison. See, among other things, original works by Donatello or Michelangelo → p. 51

● **Rainy retail therapy**
The idyllic *Borgo San Jacopo* → p. 70 is home to extravagant fashion boutiques. One shopping street which is fun whatever the weather is the Via Gioberti to the east of the centre → p. 103

● **Seven museums under one roof**
At one time, the Grand Dukes of the Medici family – and for a short period also the Italian royal family – lived here. Today, the *Palazzo Pitti* contains seven of the city's most famous museums → p. 55

● **Countryside in the rain**
The Tuscan landscape can be charming, even in rainy weather; for example when you look at it through the picture windows of the *Restaurant Omero,* over a delicious *bistecca alla fiorentina* → p. 65

● **Dazzling colours on dull days**
On entering the salesroom of the *Antico Setificio Fiorentino,* you will be overwhelmed by the glow and sparkle of the fabrics on display: velvet, silk, brocade and taffeta in every possible colour (photo, above) → p. 79

● **Art in the Renaissance palace**
Regardless of whether it's modern art or the old masters, the exhibitions in the fine rooms of the *Palazzo Strozzi* are always of the highest quality → p. 36

● **Symbol of Florentine power**
The *cathedral* is still one of the largest churches in the world with a truly stunning interior – come rain or shine → p. 29

RAIN

RELAX AND CHILL OUT
Take it easy and spoil yourself

● *Modern spa in an old palazzo*
SoulSpace is an elegant, stylish spa in the Palazzo Galletti. Treat your-self to an aroma massage or a hot stone day. A Hammam bath and a pool round off the total relaxation package → **p. 58**

● *Break with a view*
High above the busy Piazza della Repubblica you can recover from all that shopping stress over a cappuccino or a snack on the roof terrace of the *Rinascente* department store → **p. 75**

● *Soothing waters in the Giardino di Boboli*
The hectic pace of the city is forgotten in an instant when you stroll in the *Giardino di Boboli* to the sound of splashing fountains, on shady paths between statues, nymphs and grottos (photo, below) → **p. 54**

● *Monks' chanting*
The atmosphere in the *San Miniato al Monte* church is one of reflection and becomes positively meditative if you visit at around 5.30 pm. At this time, you can hear the Gregorian vespers chants coming from the neighbouring monastery → **p. 59**

● *Relax in right royal style*
The exclusive *spa at the Four Seasons hotel* has furnishings fit for a king. Even if you can't afford to stay at this luxury address, you can at least let yourself be correspondingly pampered → **p. 92**

● *Aromatherapy in the park*
In the summer, when the huge wisteria pergola is clad in blossom and the scent of iris, azaleas and hydrangeas captivates your senses, a stroll through the *Giardino Bardini* is as good as any aromatherapy session → **p. 99**

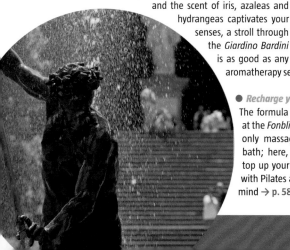

● *Recharge your batteries*
The formula for wellbeing at the *Fonbliù* includes not only massage or Turkish bath; here, you can also top up your energy levels with Pilates and clear your mind → **p. 58**

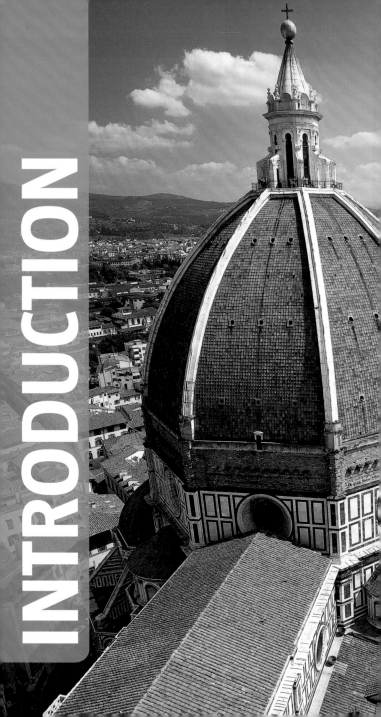

INTRODUCTION

DISCOVER FLORENCE!

Florence is a miniature metropolis and one of the most beautiful cities in the world. Young and old, singles and couples, art lovers, gourmets, shopaholics and globetrotters – everyone loves Florence!

The city centre is largely pedestrianised. Almost all major sights are easily reached on foot, without the sound of car engines disturbing your stroll through the picturesque streets and alleyways. This may sound like a lot of walking, but it really is worth every effort to see the many varied delights of this city. After Venice, Florence has to cope with the largest number of tourists per square metre of its centre. It is not difficult, though, to escape the stream of visitors. Be courageous and turn a corner into one of the side streets or tiny alleyways either side of the main thoroughfares. The city centre is small. And if you should ever get lost, you can ask any Florentine the way to the *duomo*, the cathedral. It is never far away – and, before you know it, you are back among the tourist masses once again!

Photo: Florence Cathedral

Florence has something for everyone, regardless of interests or tastes. Young people soak up the sun on the squares and gather round to listen to street musicians in the evening, stand around chatting outside the bars and trattorias, or party in the clubs. Gourmets throng to the restaurants and enoteche (wine bars) to make their informed selection of ham, cheese, wine and olive oil. Well-to-do Asians, Americans and Europeans gladly bear the burden of their purchases, acquired on the elegant shopping streets. And, sooner or later, they all end up together in the queue to get into the Uffizi Gallery, the Palazzo Pitti or the Galleria dell'Accademia. After all, Florence is all about art. The ensemble of churches and palaces, squares and alleyways, fountains and statues is a gigantic work of art, which has grown over centuries and is unequalled the world over. The finest sculptures, paintings and tapestries are on display in the churches and over 70 museums in the city. The palaces have been transformed by generations of residents into veritable treasure chambers, the majority surrounded by magnificent gardens. Many of them are open to the public. Every palace door, window ledge or roof gutter is a work of art in its own right. Let your gaze roam as you pass through the streets. You will discover much that is beautiful and interesting – things which don't even get a mention in the travel guides!

A work of art, centuries in the making

Evening on the Piazza della Signoria, Florence's profane heart

Florence's situation is also without equal. The River Arno flows through the centre of the city, and the surrounding hills are dotted with spectacular villas encircled by cypress trees. In winter and spring you can see the snow-capped peaks of the Pratomagno and the Apennines to the east and north of the city. During the building boom of recent years, wise urban planners have seen to it that the centuries-old face of the city has not changed too much. Today, only a small proportion of the 370,000 inhabitants

Seven million overnight stays per year

of Florence actually live in the centre, as housing prices are among the highest in Italy. You are more likely to meet Florentines here on their way to work or – a rare enough occurrence – shopping in the expensive boutiques. The heart of the city is in the hand of the tourists; Florence has little industry and lives to a large extent from its foreign guests. Numbers of visitors have risen again in the last few years, since now the Chinese, Russians and Eastern Europeans have discovered the city as a holiday destination. In 2010, almost seven million overnight stays were registered! On average, tourists stay in the city for three days – enough time to put together a varied programme including the most important sights yet still leaving room to soak up the city's flair. Don't rush things: plan to look at only one of the large museums and no more than two churches per day, to allow time for just strolling along and taking in your surroundings. And then look forward to the evenings, when you can savour the famous Tuscan cuisine and the region's no less famous wines at one of the many trattorias and restaurants.

What makes Florence so fascinating is, above all, its wealth of unique artistic and architectural treasures. There is scarcely another place in which so many world-famous artists have lived and worked. It is almost impossible to list all the painters, sculptors, architects, poets and philosophers who have helped to shape the face of the city down the centuries and thus contributed to its fame. The first artistic highpoint was during the 14th and 15th centuries, for example, when Dante wrote his Divine Comedy and Giotto, Orcagna and Masaccio painted their stunning frescos in the churches. Brunelleschi built the magnificent cathedral dome and Alberti formulated the theoretical principles of Renaissance art. Many others were to follow; the city flourished once again in the 16th century, thanks to the activities of Michelangelo, Raphael and Vasari.

At the height of its fortunes, Florence influenced politics, trade and art in the whole of Europe. Even then, the city was able to look back on more than 2000 years of history. Archaeological discoveries prove that a settlement must have existed here as early as the Villanova era around 1000 BC. In 59 BC, the Romans founded a veterans' colony in the Arno valley which they called *Florentia*. The forum was on the same spot as the Piazza della Repubblica today. The Romans were succeeded by the Lombards and the Carolingians, and in the year 845 AD, Lothar, grandson of Charlemagne, united the earldoms of Florence and Fiesole. Back in 1115, Florence was to all intents and purposes already an autonomous community, and the foundations for its rise to glory had already been laid. The Baptistery and the San Miniato and Santissimi Apostoli churches were built and from the 13th century onwards, Florence developed into a major European trading centre. The city had become rich and powerful, not least thanks to its flourishing textile trade and the minting of the *fiorino* in 1252. This first gold coin was to become the principle means of payment in the whole of Europe. The banking system as we know it today also has its roots in Florence. The *banco*, or money lenders' table, gave rise to the term 'bank', and it was in Florence that the first bills of exchange and cheques were issued. Florentine bankers financed the activities of popes and kings. In the city itself, a veritable building boom ensued, as churches and palaces sprang up everywhere. In 1296, following construction of the Bargello and the Palazzo Vecchio, the ruling council of this city-state of 100,000 inhabitants decided to build the mighty cathedral.

Medieval heyday – even the banks are a Florentine invention

At around this time, the rise began of the family which was destined to control the fate of the city for the next 300 years: the Medicis. Their wealth and their appreciation and sponsorship of the arts determined to a considerable extent the development and appearance of the city. Florence owes the Medici many of its most important buildings, for example, the Palazzo Medici Riccardi, residence of Cosimo il Vecchio (the Elder) with its wonderful Gozzoli Chapel. Similarly, the Basilica San Lorenzo, including the Cappella dei Principi, the family mausoleum which is entirely decorated in frescos and semi-precious stones. The Galleria degli Uffizi, too, with its world-famous collection of paintings or the Palazzo Pitti and the treasures it contains are the fruits of Medici patronage. Their spectacular villas in the immediate vicinity of the city are crowd-pullers to this day. And it was a woman, Anna Maria Luisa (1667–1743), the last of this powerful dynasty, who laid down in her will that, 'of the things which are for the decoration of the city, for the benefit of the public or a source of curiosity for outsiders (!), none should ever be sold or removed from the confines of the Grand Duchy'. As if she had foreseen the attraction the city would exert and the significance of the collections as a source of revenue in the future.

In 1737, the Grand Duchy of Tuscany fell to the house of Habsburg-Lorraine, which ruled the region, apart from a short Napoleonic intermezzo (1799–1815) until 1859. In 1861, Tuscany became part of a united Italy and between 1865 and 1871 Florence was the capital of the newly founded kingdom. This was the beginning of a second

Built for Lorenzo il Magnifico: Villa Medicea in Poggio a Caiano to the west of Florence

Renaissance for Florence. In order to underline the city's new prominence, the buildings in the old market quarter and the ghetto, which had been in existence since the Middle Ages, were torn down to make way for the Piazza della Repubblica. The massive city wall was razed to the ground and the broad ring road constructed in its place – still one of the most important thoroughfares to this day. Bourgeois quarters were founded outside this former city boundary. The course of today's Florence was charted.

For many years, the city lived exclusively from the prestige of its past. Increasingly, however, modernity is gaining a foothold. Many of the

Modernity with a historical backdrop

more recent exhibitions focus on the present or future. There is a sense of 'blowing away the cobwebs' and daring to be a little more experimental. Nowadays, anything goes – from avant-garde theatre to diverse performances – and is actively encouraged. The historic squares form the stunning backdrop to modern installations and street festivals. Considering the degree of artistic sensitivity the city has developed down the centuries, the Florence is sure to keep on thrilling its visitors in the future. After all, Florence is a metropolis – albeit a small one – but one with class and flair. And it's fun – for everyone!

WHAT'S HOT

1 Coffee culture

More than just beans In some cafés in the city you can also take in a vernissage, book presentation or a bit of theatre. There are regular readings at the *Meykadeh Libreria Café (Via dei Pepi 14r; www.meykadeh.net; photo, left)*; the *La Cité Libreria Café (Borgo San Frediano 20r; www.lacitelibreria.info)* is known for its book selection and cabaret shows; at the *Libreria Leggere Per,* there's no shortage of cultural activities, either *(Via Pippo Spano 10b; www.leggereper.it)*.

City beach

Beach without the sea You don't have to be on the coast to play beach volleyball in Florence. The *Beach Games* on the Piazzale Michelangelo see to that *(www.p3rsport.com; photo, right)*. Florentines can also get a whiff of the beach ambience at the *Lungarno Beach* under the Ponte San Niccolò on the Arno. Here, there's not only beach volleyball, but also yoga sessions and sun loungers. If you're still hunting for the right outfit for your visit to the city beach, you're sure to find something at *Sarallo Sport (Viale dei Mille 70r; www.sarallo.com)*.

3 Slow art

Don't rush it Allow yourself time to enjoy Florence, for example with *Mercurio*. Their city tours are a feast for the senses; sniff your way round the city's many aromas *(www.mercurio-italy.org; photo, left)*! If you want to take an unhurried look at the art of the Florentine masters, you could visit a fresco workshop and discover what's behind this craft *(www.contexttravel.com)*. At least once a year, Florence and its visitors drop down a gear and celebrate *Slow Art Day* looking at works of art and talking about them in groups over a meal *(www.slowartday.com)*.

Santo Spirito

Tradition meets modernity Explore the two faces of Santo Spirito. This quarter manages like no other to combine the traditional and the modern. Alongside old, established craft workshops, you'll find cool galleries and shops, too. Start your tour of the neighbourhood at the *Centro Machiavelli*. Here, shoes and mosaics are still produced by hand *(Piazza Santo Spirito 4; www.centromachiavelli.it; photo, right)*. Up-to-the-minute creations are the speciality of the three sisters at *Quelle Tre*. In their atelier, they sell quirky clothes and accessories *(Via Santo Spirito 42r)*. After your successful foray to the shops, your meal on the wooden benches at the *Osteria Santo Spirito,* with a view over the market, tastes twice as good *(Piazza Santo Spirito 16r)*.

City gardeners & eco chefs

Green is the colour Unfortunately, Florence used to be known for its poor air quality. For some years now, the city's 'green lung' has been getting larger, thanks also to the *Guerilla Gardeners (www.guerrillagardener.it)*. They have taken it into their own hands to make the city greener and are campaigning for mobile gardens on the Via dell'Agnolo and the Piazza Tasso. Fancy a 'green' holiday in Florence? Hire an environmentally friendly *Pedicab (www.pedicabfirenze.it)* and round off your eco-sightseeing tour with a visit to *La Raccolta*. This eco-restaurant has some of the most delicious food in town *(Via Giacomo Leopardi 2r)*. Right next door is *Insoliti Tessuti*, source of cool eco-friendly clothes and cosmetics *(Via Giacomo Leopardi 4r)*.

IN A NUTSHELL

CALCIO STORICO

It becomes abundantly clear that football *(calcio)* has been a Florentine passion since the 16th century, when *Calcio in Costume* is played to celebrate the city's patron, San Giovanni (24 June). Some people even maintain that the pushing and shoving of the 54 men on the Piazza S. Croce is a throw-back to *harpastum* which was played here by the Ancient Romans. Every year you notice how times – and the rules – have changed with regard to *calcio* today; the boundless enthusiasm of the Florentines, however, has not lessened down the centuries. Even now, many new-born baby girls are christened 'Viola' in honour of the football club *La Fiorentina*, nicknamed *La Viola* after the team colours.

CHINATOWN

Florence doesn't have its own Chinatown yet, but natives of this Far Eastern country are well and truly part of the fabric of the city. Today, almost 30,000 Chinese live in Florence and the surrounding area – and the figure is rising. In the city centre especially, new shops are opening daily, with clothes and fabrics fluttering outside and shelves inside packed with fashionable items. Everything is unbelievably cheap and boasts a 'Made in Italy' label, although manufactured in China.

CONTEMPORARY ART

For a long time, art in Florence meant its inheritance from the Gothic and Renaissance eras. Thankfully, mo-

Photo: Historic costume is de rigueur at the Calcio in Costume

Aspects of a multi-faceted city – Interesting facts about the Medici, Calcio Storico or the Chinese

dernity is now getting a look-in, too. Henry Moore was the first artist to successfully draw attention to modern art with a stunning exhibition at the Forte Belvedere in 1972; visitors were enthralled. Moore presented the city with a sculpture which, following much discussion, found its final position in front of the Cappella dei Pazzi (Pazzi Chapel) in Santa Croce. In the meantime, many sculptures, including works by Giò Pomodoro, Michelangelo Pistoletto, Fernando Botero, Jean-Michel Folon, Mario Ceroli

and Romano Costi, have been erected on public squares. The so-called Galleria d'Arte Moderna in the Palazzo Pitti is devoted to recent Italian art history. Above all, Tuscan paintings from the 19th and 20th centuries are on display here. The first museum for modern art was opened in 1988 – in the Romanesque church of San Pancrazio, of all places. The exhibition shows works by the sculptor and graphic artist Marino Marini. Since then, no further large museum for modern or contemporary art has been opened in

Florence. However, a handful of smaller initiatives have sparked interest with their exhibitions of modern works. The year 2009 saw the inauguration of the Centro per l'Arte Contemporanea EX3, a centre for contemporary art in the south of the city, which hosts exhibitions of international art of the present day *(www.ex3.it)*. The basement of the Palazzo Strozzi is home to the Centro di Cultura Contemporanea Strozzina, which has made a name for itself for its committed programme of exhibitions, installations, films, videos, workshops and performances *(www.strozzina.org)*.

FLORENTINE FASHION

Most visitors are struck immediately by the Florentines' elegance and dress sense. It's no wonder: Florence was known back in the Renaissance for its textiles and leather goods. The fabrics were exclusive, the shoes and bags stylish and outstandingly crafted. Renowned fashion designers of more recent years, such as Emilio Pucci, Guccio Gucci, Salvatore Ferragamo or Emilio Coveri, still profit from this reputation.

In 1951, Italy's first fashion show took place in Florence. Conte Gian Battista Giorgini, one of the most fervent supporters of the 'Made in Italy' concept, organised the event for a select few. It caused a real stir internationally and paved the way for the shows which take place every year in the Palazzo Pitti. From then on, Italy never looked back in its quest to dominate the world of fashion. Organisational problems in Florence led ultimately to the centre of Italian women's fashion being moved to Milan, though Italian menswear is still

COURSES

Whether it's language, painting, ceramics or the art of cooking you are looking for, the range of courses on offer is extremely varied. *Florenceart* **(129 D4)** *(𝄞 E6)* offers short decorative painting and trompe l'oeil courses *(Via del Campuccio 23r | www.florenceart.net)*. There's a huge selection of courses, too, at the *Florence Academy of Art* **(130 B3)** *(𝄞 H5)* *(Via delle Casine 21r | www.wflorenceacademyofart.com)*. Mario Pachioli **(126 A4)** *(𝄞 G2)* teaches painting, drawing and sculpture *(Viale Milton 49 | www.mariopachioli.it)*. An excellent place to learn various graphic-art techniques is *Il Bisonte* **(130 B4)** *(𝄞 G6)* *(Via San Niccolò 24r | www.ilbisonte.it)*. At the famous school *Palazzo Spinelli* **(129 E3)** *(𝄞 E6)* you can take summer courses and learn the craft of restoring different materials *(Istituto per l'Arte e il Restauro | Via Maggio 13 | www.spinelli.it)*. *Le Arti Orafe* **(129 D3)** *(𝄞 E6)* rates as the best goldsmith's school far and wide *(Via dei Serragli 104–124 | www.artiorafe.it)*. If you are interested in fashion, take a summer course at the renowned *Polimoda* **(128 B2)** *(𝄞 C5)* school *(Via Pisana 77 | www.polimoda.com)*. At *Cordon Bleu* **(130 B2)** *(𝄞 G5)* they'll let you into the secrets of the art of good cooking *(Via di Mezzo 55r | www.cordonbleu-it.com)*. Brush up your Italian at the British Institute of Florence (www.britishinstitute.it), the *Centro Koinè* (www.koinecenter.com), the *Istituto Il David* (www.davidschool.com) or at the *Lorenzo de' Medici* (www.ldminstitute.com).

The Medicis shaped Florence: Equestrian statue for Cosimo I in front of the Palazzo Vecchio

successfully presented in Florence every spring and autumn at the 'Pitti Uomo' fair *(www.pittimmagine.com)* (now in the Fortezza da Basso).

FORWARD-LOOKING FLORENCE

A fresh wind has been blowing through Florence, since Matteo Renzi, Italy's youngest Mayor, took over the reins in 2009. Innovation is the buzzword; Renzi wants to make his city more liveable, for citizens and visitors alike. Since taking office, he has achieved a number of things, including the pedestrianisation of almost the entire inner-city area – a fact which is particularly relevant for tourists. Most notably, the square around the Duomo and the surrounding streets are off limits to all traffic, without exception. Now, you can really take your time, strolling

between flower tubs and benches, admiring the buildings.

In February 2010, the new *tramvia* went into service. Trams now ply the route between Santa Maria Novella and Scandicci. A second line, linking the Piazza della Libertà, the Novoli university district and the Amerigo Vespucci Airport is set to follow, and a third from the main station Santa Maria Novella to the hospital complex in Careggi is on the drawing board. Mayor Renzi is bursting with enthusiasm and full of ideas. It remains to be seen how many of them he can actually put into practice.

MEDICI

Seldom has a single family determined the fate of a city over such a long period. The dynasty's founder, Giovanni di Bicci, was a banker in Rome. In 1397, he moved his headquarters to the up-and-coming city on the Arno. His son, Cosimo (1389–1464), known as *il Vecchio* (the Elder), was keen on the arts and very ambitious. Many significant buildings were erected under his rule. His son Piero (1416–69), 'the Gouty' continued the tradition of art sponsorship.

He was succeeded by his son Lorenzo (1449–92), titled *il Magnifico* with reference to his lifestyle. In the 23 years he governed the city, he managed to conquer the entire north of Tuscany. When he died at the age of only 42, Florence was the spiritual and cultural centre of Europe. Under his successor Piero II (1472–1503), however, the power and reputation of the family dwindled and was only restored thanks to Cosimo I (1519–74). His sons Francesco I (1541–87) and Ferdinando I (1549–1609) once again assumed the roles of builders and sponsors of the arts.

MISERICORDIA (MERCY)

The Fratellanza della Misericordia was founded in 1244. The members of this brotherhood devoted themselves from the very beginning to the transport of the infirm or deceased and also the care of the sick and poor. Even up to the end of the 20th century, the *fratelli* still wore medieval-style black cassocks as they leapt into their ambulances – which stand day and night before the seat of the brotherhood on the cathedral square. To guarantee the anonymity of the wearer, each used to pull a large hood over his head to hide his features. The brothers performed their charitable service free of charge. No longer anonymous, but still receiving no payment, many well-known doctors practise in the surgery of the Misericordia, close to the cathedral (Vicolo degli Adimari 1). A real blessing, not only for the city's poorer residents, but also for students and foreigners!

RENAISSANCE

Florence is the 'capital of the Renaissance'. The most famous artists of the age were either born in the city or its environs and produced their best-known works here. They included such names as Leon Battista Alberti (1404–72), architect and writer, to whom the city owes the magnificent façade of the church of Santa Maria Novella; Sandro Botticelli (1445–1510), whose paintings are to this day among the great crowd-pullers at the Uffizi; Filippo Brunelleschi (1377–1446), architect of the cathedral dome; the famed sculptor of the

CITY SIGHTSEEING

City-Sightseeing Firenze offers two different routes which take you right through town and up into the green hills to the north and south of the river. They operate on the 'hop on – hop off' principle, so you can use the same ticket to join and leave the tours as you wish within 24 hours. The busses run every 20 or 30 minutes. Audio guides provide explanations in eight languages. Tickets and route plans are available on the bus or at your hotel. *Easter–mid-June and Oct 9am–6pm, mid-June–mid-Sept 9am–10pm | 22 euros | www.firenze.city-sightseeing.it*

early Florentine Renaissance, Donatello (around 1386–1466), whose works can be seen in the churches of Santa Croce and San Lorenzo, in the Bargello and in the Cathedral Museum. Following on from these are the creator of the 'Doors of Paradise' at the Baptistery, Lorenzo Ghiberti (1378–1455), as well as Masaccio (1401–28), founder of Italian Renaissance painting, who was responsible for the frescos in the Cappella Brancacci in Santa Maria del Carmine.

Two artists of the time are truly in a class of their own: the all-round genius Leonardo da Vinci (1452–1519), at once painter, graphic artist, natural scientist and architect. Since he was born in nearby Vinci, his works can be viewed at the local museum as well as at the Uffizi. Michelangelo (1475–1564), another figure of genius, was not only a painter, architect and poet; he was also one of the finest proponents of neo-classic sculpture. His David is one of the most photographed motifs in Florence. Yet another man who subsequently contributed greatly to the fame of the city was Giorgio Vasari (1511–74). A painter, writer and architect, he also designed the Uffizi.

STENDHAL SYNDROME

Florence is the richest city in the world in terms of art treasures – every visitor knows that. But what most of them don't know is that this can be dangerous! Watch out for the Stendhal Syndrome! The French writer Marie-Henri Stendhal described his visit to the church of Santa Croce in his travel journals, published in 1817. He was so overwhelmed by the proximity to the great men of arts and letters who lay buried there that he began to feel faint. This type of emotional hyper-sensitivity has now been termed the 'Stendhal Syndrome'. According to statistics, around a dozen visitors to the art treasures have to be treated for the syndrome in Florentine hospitals every year.

Statue by Jean-Michel Folon at the Forte Belvedere

THE PERFECT DAY
Florence in 24 hours

08:00am THE EARLY BIRD ...

... starts the day with a cappuccino! What better way to get the day going than with a brioche and a really good cappuccino at the famous *Café Rivoire* → p. 62 on the *Piazza della Signoria* → p. 38. Home to the *Palazzo Vecchio* → p. 36 and the *Loggia dei Lanzi* → p. 33, it is one of the most evocative places in Florence.

09:00am AN ARTY START TO THE MORNING

Take a walk down the Via de' Calzaiuoli past the former grain market *Orsanmichele* → p. 35 and stroll across the Piazza della Repubblica, where you can buy an English-language newspaper at the kiosk under the triumphal arch. Then you could go to the majestic *Palazzo Strozzi* → p. 36, which might just be staging an interesting art exhibition.

10:00am WHERE HIGH SOCIETY SHOPS

From the inner courtyard of the palace, you step directly onto Via Tornabuoni, the city's haute couture Mecca. As long as your purse or wallet can take the strain, you can treat yourself to a complete outfit, say, something exclusive from *Emilio Pucci* → p. 77 (photo, left) or a pair of shoes from *Salvatore Ferragamo* → p. 78.

11:00am STOP FOR A READ ON THE PIAZZA

Further westwards, you pass along the winding alleyways of medieval Florence, past the *Museo Marino Marini* → p. 46, and on the pretty Piazza Santa Maria Novella, where you could take a break on one of the benches and scan the headlines in your newspaper or soak up a little sun before visiting the *church* → p. 48 of the same name with its innumerable, fine art treasures.

12:00pm MARKET AND MEDICI

Heading back towards town again, you reach the *Cappelle Medicee* → p. 45, the impressive mausoleum of the Medici family, and the *Basilica di San Lorenzo* → p. 44. Round about, the large, bustling tourist market is a safe bet for tracking down a suitable souvenir.

01:00pm LUNCH AT THE MARKET

Now, everything depends on how hungry you are. In the market hall you can have yourself a delicious *panino* made up at one of the many stalls, or sit down to lunch at the *Trattoria Gozzi Sergio* → p. 68 opposite the church, hidden behind the market stalls. Share the atmosphere of this typical eatery with the many Florentines who come here to treat themselves to a plate of good pasta.

03:00pm TO THE CATHEDRAL

Reinvigorated, head down the Borgo San Lorenzo with its many shoe shops, coming to a halt on the square between the overwhelming *Duomo* → p. 29 and the *Battistero* → p. 28. You should also take the time to visit the *Museo dell'Opera del Duomo* → p. 34, where you can see the originals of the fascinating sculpture work created for the cathedral.

04:00pm DANTE AND DEVILISHLY GOOD ICE CREAM

Via del Proconsolo leads you away from the tourist masses. Make a detour to the *birthplace of Dante Alighieri* → p. 29 (photo, centre), before strolling along the Borgo degli Albizi. You're sure to cross paths with people licking ice creams, on their way back from *Vivoli* → p. 63 (photo, right) – the best ice cream parlour in town.

05:00pm THE PANTHEON OF FLORENCE

Just a few steps further on, like a theatre backdrop, the Piazza Santa Croce opens out before you to present the glorious *Basilica di Santa Croce* → p. 52, main church of the Franciscans and 'Pantheon of Florence'. If you hurry, you have until 5.30 pm to get to the leather workshop *Scuola del Cuoio* → p. 76, where the clientele includes the King of Morocco and the English nobility. After that, it's time for an aperitivo at *Moyo* → p. 82.

08:00pm AND FINALLY ...

... bring the day to a resounding close with a *bistecca alla fiorentina* in the *Osteria dei Pazzi* → p. 67. Or take another dose of culture with, perhaps, a stage performance at the historic Baroque *Teatro della Pergola* → p. 85.

Distance: approx. 2.5 mi
Go without breakfast at the hotel and enjoy watching Florence rub the sleep out of its eyes instead!

SIGHTSEEING

CITY **WHERE TO START?**

Ponte Vecchio (122 B–C5)
(*F5*): Stand on the famous Arno bridge and get your bearings; heading out of town, you come to the mighty Palazzo Pitti and the Via Maggio with its many antique dealers. On the other side of the river you can see the Uffizi. Behind them come the Piazza della Signoria with the city landmark, the Palazzo Vecchio, and a little to the northeast, the Piazza della Repubblica and the Piazza del Duomo. Electric minibuses C3 and D; car parking at the main railway station, Santa Maria Novella

If you want to appreciate the beauty of Florence in its entirety, you should time your visit for the early morning, when only the street-cleaning vehicles trundle along the streets and no crowds block your view of the architectural ensemble. Florence is best explored on foot – no problem, since almost all the sights are within the square mile of the city centre! Generally speaking, the churches are open from 8am–12.30pm and 3pm or 4pm–6pm. **INSIDER TIP** Have a handful of coins at the ready: you'll need them to feed the 'talking info posts' and to switch on the floodlights in the chapels!

The museum landscape in Florence is infinitely varied: Besides the universally acclaimed art collections at the Uffizi

Photo: Galleria degli Uffizi

Art, as far as the eye can see – blockbuster museums, glorious churches and fabulous palaces await your visit

and the Palazzo Pitti, it's worth taking a look at the Museo Nazionale del Bargello and the Galleria dell'Accademia, which house important sculptures, as well as the host of museums scattered across the city dedicated to science and other disciplines. Please note that admission to churches, museums and parks is generally no longer possible 30 minutes or one hour before closing time.

You can get an overall idea of the state museums and what they have to offer from *www.firenzemusei.it*, while *www.museifiorentini.it* has information on the municipal museums. To avoid long queues, come to Florence in the winter if you can, or reserve admission tickets to the state museums in advance *(at least 5 days before your visit! | www.firenze musei.it or www.florence-museum.com | Booking fee: approx. 5 euros, for special exhibitions, add another 3 euros).*

Whatever you do, wear comfortable shoes! Pavements are often narrow, old

The map shows the location of the most interesting districts. There is a detailed map of each district on which each of the sights described is numbered.

and unevenly paved. Just start walking! Florence is small, and as the dome of the cathedral is visible from almost every direction, it's practically impossible to get lost.

SOUTHERN SAN GIOVANNI

The area between the Duomo and Palazzo Vecchio, the seat of local government, is the centre of the city. Where Romans once marched along the *Cardo Maximus*, hordes of tourists jostle along today's *Via Calzaiuoli*.

Since time immemorial, this street full of fashion boutiques and shoe shops, ice cream parlours and obligatory pizzerias, has linked the secular and profane sides of the city. This is the nerve-centre of Florence, and everyone passes this way – even the hastiest tourist.

■ BATTISTERO DI SAN GIOVANNI
(122 C3) (*ⓜ F4*)

The octagonal baptistery is clad on the outside in white and green marble; inside, it impresses above all thanks to the large INSIDERTIP Byzantine mosaic under the dome and the fine 12th-century mosaic flooring. The three *bronze portals* leading into the building deserve closer inspection. The most famous is the one facing the cathedral, the *Porta del Para-*

diso (Door of Paradise), which took the craftsmen in Lorenzo Ghiberti's workshop 26 years to complete (1426–52). Ten bronze panels depict scenes from the Old Testament. The bald-headed figure in the right-hand column of the door's left wing is a self-portrait of Ghiberti. A number of the reliefs were swept away when the Arno flooded the city in 1966 and were replaced with copies. The door now shines once again, having been re-gilded. The restored original panels are in the cathedral museum. Also by Lorenzo Ghiberti, the *north portal* features 28 panels. The oldest door is the *south portal*, on which Andrea Pisano illustrated the spiritual and secular virtues between 1330 and 1336. *Mon–Sat 12.15pm–7pm, Sun and 1st Sat in the month 8.30am–2pm | Admission: 4 euros | Piazza S. Giovanni | www.operaduomo.firenze.it*

2 CASA DI DANTE (123 D4) (*ffl F5*)

This medieval house is named after Dante Alighieri, who is assumed to have been born here. Its three storeys showcase various editions of his Divina Commedia as well as documents relating to his political and literary life and exile in Ravenna. *Oct–March Tue–Sun 10am–5pm, April–Sept daily 10am–6pm | Admission: 4 euros | Via S. Margherita 1 | www.museocasadidante.it*

3 DUOMO DI SANTA MARIA DEL FIORE & CAMPANILE ★ ●
(122–123 C–D3) (*ffl F–G4*)

The massive cupola of the cathedral dominates the Florence skyline for miles around. Its construction was what you might call a belated triumph, since Pisa, Lucca, Pistoia, Prato and Siena already had their own magnificent cathedrals by the time Florence city council finally got round to commissioning the building of this one in 1296. The task was assigned to Arnolfo di Cambio, and the gigantic project was completed in 1368,

MARCO POLO HIGHLIGHTS

admittedly without the ● *cupola*. It was not until the next century that this was added by Filippo Brunelleschi (1420–34). The planned diameter of the dome was over 45 m and presented considerable, hitherto unknown constructional challenges. Brunelleschi's concept was based essentially on the fact that bodies which lean towards each other support each other too. He therefore built inner and outer concentric domes resting on the drum of the cathedral.

If you feel up to it, climb the 463 steps up to the ⚜ lantern through the nave and the double-walled cupola – the same route taken by the construction workers of old! (Caution: one-way system – it's not possible to turn around and go back!) On the way, you get a fascinating insight into the INSIDER TIP 'innards' of the dome – and ultimately an amazing view of the city!

Florence Cathedral is the fourth-largest church in Christendom. Its surface area is 8300 m² (9926.9yd²), at a length of 160 m (175yd); the nave is 43 m (47yd) wide, the transept, 90 m. Many re-nowned Florentine artists contributed at the time to its decoration. The large fresco (the second on the left-hand side) shows the equestrian statue of mercenary leader Sir John Hawkwood, who once triumphed in battle for the city. It was painted in 1436 by Paolo Uccello and served as the model for all subsequent works of its kind. The painting of the equestrian statue of Niccolò da Tolentino next to it is by Andrea del Castagno (1456). The circular stained-glass windows in the drum at the base of the dome are also very beautiful and were designed by a number of major artists of the 14th century. The inside of the dome was embellished with frescos depicting the *Last Judgement* by Giorgio Vasari and Federico Zuccari between 1572 and 1579. The colourful, glazed *terracotta reliefs* above the entrances to the two Sacristies are by Luca della Robbia (1444–69), as is the *bronze door* to the New Sacristy to the left of the high altar. The famous cantorias ('singing galleries') by Donatello and Luca della Robbia as well as the *Pietà* by Michelangelo can now be seen

Panorama guaranteed after 414 steps: You can climb the campanile as well as the dome of the duomo

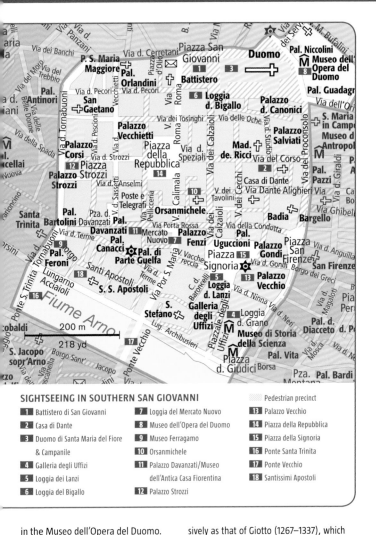

SIGHTSEEING IN SOUTHERN SAN GIOVANNI

1. Battistero di San Giovanni
2. Casa di Dante
3. Duomo di Santa Maria del Fiore & Campanile
4. Galleria degli Uffizi
5. Loggia dei Lanzi
6. Loggia del Bigallo
7. Loggia del Mercato Nuovo
8. Museo dell'Opera del Duomo
9. Museo Ferragamo
10. Orsanmichele
11. Palazzo Davanzati/Museo dell'Antica Casa Fiorentina
12. Palazzo Strozzi
13. Palazzo Vecchio
14. Piazza della Repubblica
15. Piazza della Signoria
16. Ponte Santa Trinita
17. Ponte Vecchio
18. Santissimi Apostoli

Pedestrian precinct

in the Museo dell'Opera del Duomo.

A staircase to the right of the main entrance leads down into the remains of the Early Christian church of *Santa Reparata*, which pre-dates the cathedral and which was uncovered in 1966. It contains the tomb of Brunelleschi, among others. In 2000, a skeleton found there was identified conclu-

sively as that of Giotto (1267–1337), which was then laid to rest next to Brunelleschi. The exterior of the cathedral is clad in white Carrara marble and green marble from Prato. The front section of the façade was only completed in 1887 in the neo-Gothic style. Directly next to the cathedral stands the *campanile* (bell tower), which was

designed by Giotto and built between 1334 and 1359. Due to his harmonious proportions and use of colour, it rates as one of the most beautiful in Italy. Its façade features encrustations of white, red and green marble. The lower section has 54 bas-reliefs from the school of Andrea Pisano; in the niches above stand statues of the saints, prophets and sibyls by artists such as Donatello (the originals are also in the Museo dell'Opera del Duomo). The climb up the *campanile* is not overly strenuous: 414 well-proportioned steps lead up to the balustrade of the flat roof and to a fabulous panorama. *Duomo: Mon–Fri 10am–5pm, Thu until approx. 4pm, Sat until 4.45pm, Sun 1.30pm–4.45pm; dome: Mon–Fri 8.30am–7pm, Sat until 5.40pm | Admission: 8 euros; campanile: daily 8.30am–7.30pm | Admission: 6 euros; S. Reparata crypt: Mon–Wed, Fri 10am–5pm, Thu until approx. 4pm, Sat until 4.45pm | Admission: 3 euros | www.operaduomo.firenze.it*

▣ GALLERIA DEGLI UFFIZI ★ ●
(122 C5) (*⌖ F5*)

Commissioned by Cosimo I de' Medici, the building was constructed according to plans by Giorgio Vasari between 1559 and 1581 to house the city's administrative offices ('uffizi' in Italian). Meanwhile, the 39 rooms on the upper floor of the *Galleria degli Uffizi* are home to one of the richest and most fabled painting collections in the world. The second floor contains the *Gabinetto dei Disegni e delle Stampe*, a collection of 104,000 drawings and prints. The floors below are gradually being converted into exhibition space – the *Nuovi Uffizi* ('New Uffizi'). (You can follow the progress of this enormous project under *www.nuoviuffizi.it*.) The objective is not only to reorganise the presentation of works currently on display, but to find room for many of the art treasures which have been hidden from view in the storerooms for years.

The paintings in the museum are arranged chronologically and according to schools. The main emphasis is on the Italian Renaissance. Greek and Roman statues as well as Flemish Gobelin tapestries are to be seen in the corridors from which the various rooms lead off. The most valuable statues stand on specially constructed plinths in the *Tribuna*, the magnificent octagonal room which was one of the first to be conceived as a backdrop for works of art.

Following the signposts for a suggested tour you come first to the large Gothic altarpieces by Cimabue and Giotto, followed by works from the Sienese school of the 14th century and the great painters of the early Renaissance: Masaccio, Piero della Francesca and also Sandro Botticelli, whose paintings, including *The Birth of Venus*, are displayed in their own room. Leonardo da Vinci's masterpieces on display here include the unfinished *Adoration of the Magi*. The above-men-

The finest open-air museum in the city – the Loggia dei Lanzi

tioned *Tribuna* contains not only precious statues, but above all portraits of the Medici family by Bronzino, Pontormo and other representatives of the Mannerist school. In rooms XIX–XXIII, some of the earliest to function as galleries, are devoted to other Renaissance artworks. The west wing of the building contains works by Michelangelo *(Tondo Doni)*, Raphael *(The Madonna of the Goldfinch)*, Titian *(Venus of Urbino)* as well as by the Venetian artists Veronese, Giorgione, Tintoretto and Caravaggio. Next up are the Dutch painters, including Rubens (Portrait of Isabella Brandt), Rembrandt and van Dyck. Between rooms XXV and XXIV is the door to the Corridoio Vasariano, a passageway almost 1 km (0.62mi) long which links the Uffizi and the Palazzo Pitti via the Ponte Vecchio. It is decorated with almost 1000 paintings, among them many self-portraits *(closed for renovation work until 2014)*.

If the prospect of 'going it alone' through the Uffizi is too daunting, you can take an official guided tour. *Tue–Sun 8.15am– 6.50pm | Admission: 6.50 euros, special exhibitions: 10 euros | Loggiato degli Uffizi 6 | www.uffizi.com*

■5 LOGGIA DEI LANZI ● (122 C5) *(ØØ F5)*

As early as 1376–82, the city council, the *Signoria*, had the loggia built for receptions and other ceremonial occasions. It is thought by some to have been designed by Orcagna, for which reason it is also sometimes referred to as the *Loggia dell'Orcagna;* its more commonly used name today, *Loggia dei Lanzi,* harks back to the days when Cosimo I's German mercenaries, the *lanzichenecchi* (so-called *Landsknechte*) were stationed here. Similarly, its location on the Piazza della Signoria gives it its third designation, the *Loggia della Signoria.*

With its three majestic round arches, the loggia is a prime example of Florentine Gothic. Cosimo I had two groups of figures erected to symbolise the triumph of the rule of force over democracy: the carefully restored bronze composition *Perseus with the Head of Medusa* (1545–54), a masterpiece by Benvenuto Cellini, stands in all its former glory and in its original position (the marble plinth is a copy; the original is in the Museo Nazionale del Bargello). The Mannerist work of intertwined figures *The Rape of the Sabines,* a little further to the right, is by Giambologna (1583). Further sculptures, including six statues of Roman women along the rear wall, complete the decorative picture.

In 1583, a famous hanging garden was laid out on the roof of the loggia; today it is the site of a 🍴 café which is accessible from the Uffizi and from which you have a marvellous view across the piazza. *Piazza della Signoria*

6 LOGGIA DEL BIGALLO (122 C3) (*(ω F5)*)

On the corner of the Piazza S. Giovanni near the cathedral, lay brethren would let unwanted and orphaned children play underneath their loggia, with the aim of finding parents for them. The *Fratellanza della Misericordia,* founded in 1244, had commissioned the late Gothic building in 1352. In 1425, the brotherhood united with the Compagnia di Santa Maria del Bigallo, which gave its name to the loggia. Downstairs is the surgery of the *Misericordia* emergency doctors who offer their services free of charge. The upper floor houses a small, but informative, exhibition on the activities of the order. *Wed–Mon 10am–2pm and 3pm–6.50pm | Admission: 5 euros | Piazza S. Giovanni 1 | www.bigallo.net*

7 LOGGIA DEL MERCATO NUOVO (122 C4) (*(ω F5)*)

The arches of this open, colonnaded walkway were a favourite venue in Florence of the 14th to 16th centuries for private meetings and public market dealings. Gold and silver were once traded here; today, straw artefacts, tablecloths and all kinds of cheap bric-a-brac. The best thing about the 'New Market' is the architecture of this 1547 loggia which is best appreciated on Sundays and Mondays during the winter months when the stalls have vanished. Tourists are attracted to the bronze statue of a wild boar, *il porcellino* on the south side of the loggia. The original is in the Museo Bardini; its marble prototype in the Uffizi. Toss a coin in the fountain and stroke the piglet's snout and you are sure to return to the city, it is said! *Via Porta Rossa/Via Por Santa Maria*

8 INSIDER TIP MUSEO DELL'OPERA DEL DUOMO (123 D3) (*(ω G4–5)*)

Here, you can see the originals of those sculptures which now stand as replicas in the cathedral, baptistery and campanile as well as various tools, plans and models connected with their construction. Michelangelo's famous Pietà is here too. *Mon–Sat 9am–7.30pm, Sun 9am–*

LOW BUDGET

▶ Admission charges to museums are relatively high, but EU residents under 25 pay half-price in the state museums in Florence; the over-65s get in free (don't forget your ID!).

▶ For one week in the spring, all state museums in Italy are open to the public free of charge. Information offices in the city have details of the exact dates.

▶ During the international music festival *Maggio Musicale Fiorentino* in May and June you can sit in for free on the amazing rehearsals in various concert venues, usually on Sunday mornings. More information at *www. maggiofiorentino.com*

1.40pm | Admission: 6 euros | Piazza del Duomo | www.operaduomo.firenze.it

9 MUSEO FERRAGAMO
(122 B4) (𝄞 F5)

The rooms on the lower floors of the Palazzo Spini Feroni tell the story of the city's guilds in 1336 to build a new church. The open arcades of the ground floor – alongside functioning as a place of worship – also served as a market hall and the floors above as a grain store. Around the middle of the 14th century, the arcades of the loggia were closed by means

Orsanmichele looks like a palace but is actually a church

footwear maestro Salvatore Ferragamo (1927–60) and the associated brand. Thousands of pairs of shoes bear witness, and include models worn by such stars as Marilyn Monroe, Greta Garbo, Audrey Hepburn or Judy Garland. *Wed–Mon 10am–6pm | Admission: 5 euros | Piazza Santa Trinita 5r | www.museoferragamo.it*

10 ORSANMICHELE (122 C4) (𝄞 F5)

A stop-off at the church of Orsanmichele is a must for all Florence visitors. The history of this place of worship, which resembles a medieval palace rather than a church, is typical of the Florentine sense of practicality.

When the chapel of *San Michele in Orto*, dating back to the 8th century, was destroyed by fire, the *Signoria* ordered the

of triple-lancet windows, and Andrea Orcagna erected a monumental Gothic tabernacle around Bernardo Daddi's 1347 painting *Madonna delle Grazie*.

The grain market was moved in 1361 from the ground floor; the two upper floors were used as a grain store until well into the 16th century. Openings in the northern pillars indicate where, in times of food shortages, the sacks of grain were lowered down to be distributed free of charge to the needy – in the hope of warding off possible unrest in the city. Today, the upper floors are used to stage exhibitions – a good opportunity to take a look at the fine Gothic rooms. Statues of the patron saints of the guilds, fashioned by the most important Renaissance sculptors, stand in 14 niches on the

True-to-life interiors in the Palazzo Davanzati

tion of Florentine houses between the Middle Ages and the Renaissance. The brilliance of the magnificent murals in the *Sala dei Papagalli* (Parrot Room) as well as in the gentlemen's and ladies' chambers has recently been painstakingly restored. In the kitchen on the 3rd floor *(by appointment only; Tel. 05 52 38 86 10)* you can see a display of everyday household objects of the period. *Daily 8.15am–1.50pm, closed 2nd and 4th Sun as well as 1st, 3rd and 5th Mon in the month | Admission: 2 euros | Via Porta Rossa 13*

12 PALAZZO STROZZI ●
(122 B4) (*ɱ F5*)

Built for Medici rivals, the Strozzi family, this is the epitome of the Florentine Renaissance palace. No fewer than 15 houses had to be demolished in order to build this structure of roughly hewn stone on this prominent site. Construction began in 1489 under Benedetto da Maiano and was completed in 1536 by Simone del Pollaiuolo, 'il Cronaca'. He was also responsible for the generously proportioned, arcaded inner courtyards. Today, the palazzo stages top-flight art exhibitions. *Fri–Wed 9am–8pm, Thu until 11pm | Admission: 10 euros | Piazza Strozzi | www.palazzostrozzi.org*

13 PALAZZO VECCHIO ★ ☼
(123 D5) (*ɱ F5*)

This splendid, crenellated palace with its 94-m-high tower was built between 1299 and 1314 by Arnolfo di Cambio and served initially as the seat of government and living quarters of the highest officials in the Republic.

In 1540, Cosimo I turned the medieval palace into his ducal residence. The additions and conversions he had carried out created a dazzling interior, while the exterior remained largely unchanged.

church exterior. Most of the statues, including Donatello's famous *marble statue of St George*, patron saint of armourers, have been replaced with replicas. The originals are now in the *Museo Nazionale del Bargello*. *Daily 10am–5pm | Free admission | Via dell'Arte della Lana*

11 INSIDER TIP PALAZZO DAVANZATI/ MUSEO DELL'ANTICA CASA FIORENTINA ● (122 B4) (*ɱ F5*)

Discover one of the finest palaces in the city: complete with furniture, paintings and other objects, it gives a true reflec-

Giorgio Vasari was charged with overseeing the building work, though his heightened enthusiasm for the task led him to overlay certain irreplaceable works, such as Leonardo da Vinci's *Battle of Anghiari* in the Salone dei Cinquecento, with his own paintings illustrating the fame and fortune of the Medicis. The palace took on its current name, *Palazzo Vecchio* (Old Palace), when the ducal court moved to the 'new' one, the Palazzo Pitti.

The beautiful *inner courtyard,* modified in 1470 by Michelozzo, was decorated with frescos depicting Austrian cityscapes to mark the wedding of Ferdinand I and Johanna of Austria in 1565. The *Quartieri Monumentali*, the magnificent private apartments, are on the 1st floor.

The *Salone dei Cinquecento*, the Room of the Five Hundred, was originally the debating hall of the municipal council and was later converted into an audience chamber by Cosimo I. The 53.7-m-long, 22.4-m-wide and 17.8-m-high chamber (58.7yd x 25.5yd x 19.5yd) is the largest room in the city and – like the *Sala dei Dugento* also crowned by a fabulously carved wooden ceiling by Michelozzo – is still used on festive occasions. Marble statues, among them the *Genius of Victory* by Michelangelo and *Florence defeating Pisa* by Giambologna, stand in front of Vasari's monumental battle scenes along the walls.

On the 2nd floor are the *Quartieri degli Elementi* and the apartments of Eleonora di Toledo, wife of Cosimo I. The adjacent *Cappella della Signoria* was ornamented with frescos by Ghirlandaio in 1514. The *Sala dell'Udienza* is particularly impressive, with its elaborately carved ceiling and the marble doorway by Benedetto da Maiano, as is the *Sala dei Gigli*, so named because it is decorated entirely with the French emblem, the *fleur-de-lys*. In the centre of the room stands Donatello's bronze composition *Judith and Holofernes.* During his time as Secretary to the Second Chancery of the Republic, Niccoló Machiavelli worked in the *Segreteria*. Another interesting feature can be found in the *Guardaroba*, the 'Wardrobe Room', which contains cupboards painted with 53 maps from the period 1563–75. The oldest part of the palace, the former armoury *(Sala d'Arme),* today stages changing exhibitions. The entrance is on the left-hand side of the palace.

Twelve multimedia stations give you an insight into the history, art and architecture of the building. Furthermore, it is possible to take a look at previously inaccessible parts of the palace in guided tours of the so-called INSIDER TIP secret passages *(percorsi segreti)*. A bookshop and the ticket office have been relocated to the second inner courtyard,

CITY LIGHTS

The traditional sand diggers on the Arno have fitted out their boats to accommodate passengers, taking them for a peaceful, relaxing one-hour trip under the bridges of the city and regaling them with tales of past times and their arduous work. In the evenings in particular, when the palaces along the river banks are lit up, this is a delightful way to see Florence! From May to September – water levels permitting. Minimum 5 persons. *Per person: 12 euros | Tel. Info/booking through Paolo Bruni 34 77 98 23 56 | www.renaioli.it*

A domineering Neptune surveys the Piazza della Signoria from his fountain

the *Cortile della Dogana*. The entrance to the *Museo dei Ragazzi*, an excellent museum for children (and their parents), is also here. *Percorsi segreti and Museo dei Ragazzi: Mon–Sat 9.30am–5pm, Sun until 12.30pm | Supplementary charge: 2 euros | By appointment only, Tel. 05 52 76 82 24 | Piazza della Signoria, entry via the Via dei Gondi | www. palazzovecchio-familymuseum.it; Palace/ Quartieri Monumentali: Fri–Wed 9am–7pm, Thu 9am–2pm | Admission: 6 euros | Advance booking, Tel. 05 52 76 83 | Piazza della Signoria*

14 PIAZZA DELLA REPUBBLICA
(122 C3–4) (*ⓂF5*)

This location has always been a central hub in the city: first, Roman forum, then marketplace and Jewish ghetto. The square itself was created as part of the urban redevelopment which was undertaken when Florence was declared capital of the new united Italy in 1890. Today, it is lined with cafés and is the bustling heart of the business district.

15 PIAZZA DELLA SIGNORIA
(122 C4–5) (*ⓂF5*)

Dominated as it is by the fortress-like Palazzo Vecchio, the square is simply breathtaking. The *Loggia della Signoria* (Loggia dei Lanzi) and the Uffizi Galleries form the southern boundary of the piazza, on the north side is the *Palazzo Uguccioni* (1559) and on the bulging eastern flank stands the *Tribunale della Mercanzia* (Tribunal of Merchandise, 1359), whose façade is adorned with the coats of arms of the 21 guilds. The buildings opposite the palace, which house cafés and shops, were built at the end of the 19th century in a style echoing their surroundings.

The many statues and monuments scattered across the square serve to give it a pleasant, more informal atmosphere. Highlights in front of the Palazzo Vecchio include the gigantic marble figure of *David* by Michelangelo (1504, a copy; the original is in the Galleria dell'Accademia); the group *Hercules and Caco* by Baccio Bandinelli (1533) and Donatello's 1460 bronze composition *Judith and Holofernes* (copy; original in the Palazzo Vecchio). Between the imposing *Fontana de Nettuno* (Neptune Fountain) by Bartolomeo Ammanati (1565) and Giambologna's bronze *equestrian statue of Cosimo I de' Medici* (1594), a granite slab inscribed with the date 1498 is set into the ground. It marks the spot where Dominican monk Girolamo Savonarola and two of his supporters were burnt at the stake by order of the Borgia Pope Alexander VI. Every year on 23 May, the anniversary of the execution, representatives of the Church and the city lay a floral tribute here.

16 PONTE SANTA TRÍNITA ≈
(122 B5) (*F5*)

The three elegant arches of this bridge seem to step, light-footed, across the Arno. Designed by Michelangelo, it was actually built by Ammanati between 1567 and 1570. When reconstruction of the damaged bridges began at the end of World War II, the remnants of the ponte

were fished out of the river, and the quarries in the Boboli Gardens, from which the original stone came, were opened again to source material for its repair. From here, you have a sensational view downstream to the Ponte Vecchio, particularly memorable at sunset.

17 PONTE VECCHIO ★ ≈ ●
(122 B–C5) (*F5*)

The 'Old Bridge' is one of the outstanding landmarks of Florence. Even back in Etruscan times there was a river crossing point here, and Via Cassia, one of the most important Roman trade routes, led northwards along this way. The bridge as we see it today, which crosses the river at its narrowest point, was built in 1345 by Neri di Fioravanti or Taddeo Gaddi. It is characterised by the overhanging construction of the shops which line the bridge. From 1422 to 1593 it was where most of the city's butchers plied their trade. When the ducal family moved to the Palazzo Pitti, they were disturbed

SPORT-CRAZY

Almost all Florentines are *tifosi*, fans of the football team A.C.F. Fiorentina *(www.acffiorentina.it)*. Home games take place every other Sunday (info: *www.fiorentina.it*). Tickets can be bought directly at the stadium *(Stadio Comunale Artemio Franchi (127 E4) (*K3*) | Viale Manfredo Fanti 4 | Tel. 05 55 03 26 28)* or at the ticket office close to the Piazza della Repubblica *(Chiosco degli Sportivi | Via Anselmi | Tel. 0 55 29 23 63)*. Important: For security reasons, tickets are only sold upon presentation of your passport or identity card and are individually

marked with your name!

Fans of the sport with the not-so-round ball, rugby, can choose from seven clubs in and around Florence which practise this increasingly popular team game. *(Info: www.firenzerugby1931.it or www. firenzerugbyclub.it)*

Some 30 km north of Florence, in the heart of the Mugello, is the motor racing circuit of the same name. The Grand Prix, the Gran Premio d'Italia, is held here every year, as is the Formula 3000 race *(Tel. 05 58 49 91 11 | www.mugello circuit.it)*. Tickets in advance from *www. ticketone.it*.

by the stench, and Ferdinand I decreed that, from then onwards, only gold and silversmiths could conduct their business on the bridge.

Since he wanted to be able to get from the Palazzo Vecchio to the Palazzo Pitti without getting his feet wet, Cosimo I commissioned his architect Giorgio Vasari in 1565 with the building of the *Corridoio Vasariano*, which runs above the shops on the eastern side. The Ponte Vecchio was the only bridge not blown up by the German army in 1944; to spare the bridge, however, large sections of the old residential areas on either side of it were destroyed. Today, the bridge and its jeweller's boutiques is a major crowd-puller in the city.

18 SANTISSIMI APOSTOLI
(122 B5) (*F5*)

The Church of the Holy Apostles is a beautiful small parish church, set back somewhat from the well-trodden tourist routes. It was built in the 11th century in the form of an Early Christian basilica with a semi-circular apse. According to a plaque on the façade, the church was a donation of Charlemagne, though this subsequently turned out to be a myth. Some of the black-green marble columns of the interior originate from nearby Roman thermal baths. The painted roof timbering (14th century) is the best preserved of its kind in the city. A narrow passageway leads from the square in front of the church down to the riverside Lungarno degli Acciaiuoli. *Daily 10am–noon and 3.30pm–7pm | Piazza del Limbo 1*

NORTHERN SAN GIOVANNI

In recent centuries, the district to the north of the cathedral has split into two distinct areas: one surrounds the *Basilica di San Lorenzo,* with the large market hall of the same name and

Clinging like swallows' nests to the bridge, the picturesque jeweller's shops on the Ponte Vecchio

colourful stalls outside it; the other stretches from the Piazza del Duomo to San Marco and Santissima Annunziata, where the university of Florence was once situated.

Most faculties have since been relocated to Novoli, and, with the academic departments, many students have also left the area. Only the art students at the famous *Accademia di Belle Arti,* under the arcades of the busy Piazza San Marco, make for a student atmosphere. Yet northern San Giovanni has undergone even more changes in the last few years. The presence of many immigrants – whether they be recent arrivals in the city or second- or third-generation residents – has turned this into a multicultural but also rather down-at-heel district – depending on which way you look at things. Although the city's main attractions are centred San Giovanni, here in the streets to the north of the duomo, you no longer have the feeling of being surrounded only by tourists.

■ BIBLIOTECA MEDICEA LAURENZIANA
(122 C2) (*ØU F4*)

The library, which was completed in 1578, now contains one of the most valuable collections of manuscripts in the world. Michelangelo designed the architecturally most unconventional vestibule, with its grandiose INSIDER TIP *staircase,* as well as the INSIDER TIP *Sala Grande* (Main Reading Room) opening out from it. He was also responsible for the lecterns and the wooden ceiling. The pattern of the ceiling is taken up by the floor. *Mon–Sat 9.30am–1.30pm | Piazza S. Lorenzo 9, entry to the left of the church façade | www.bml.firenze.sbn.it*

■ CIMITERO DEGLI INGLESI ●
(126 B5) (*ØU H4*)

The hill raised outside the city walls became the last resting place for Florence's non-Catholic residents, in particular the English, but also Swiss, Russians and Americans. The most famous grave is that of the English poet Elizabeth Barrett Browning, who lived together with her husband Robert Browning for 14 years in Casa Guidi *(Mon/Wed/Fri 3pm–5pm | Piazza San Felice 8).* Today, the cemetery is an idyllic spot amidst the urban traffic, where you can still detect the scent of roses behind the protective barrier of cypress trees! *Winter: Tue–Fri 2pm–5pm; summer: Tue–Fri 3pm–6pm, Mon 9am–noon | Piazzale Donatello*

■ GALLERIA DELL'ACCADEMIA ★
(125 D–E1) (*ØU G4*)

The seven major works of Michelangelo are the main attraction at this gallery. The unfinished marble sculptures of the four *Prisoners,* along the walls of the main exhibition room, were intended for the tomb of Pope Julius II in Rome. The statue of *St Matthew,* Michelangelo's only figure of an Apostle destined for the

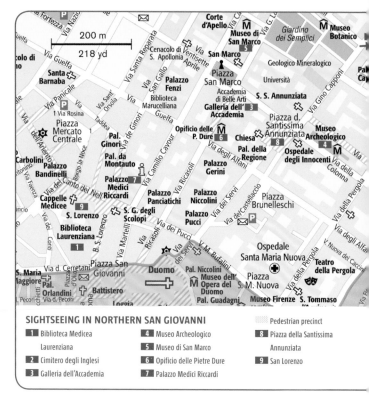

SIGHTSEEING IN NORTHERN SAN GIOVANNI

1 Biblioteca Medicea Laurenziana

2 Cimitero degli Inglesi

3 Galleria dell'Accademia

4 Museo Archeologico

5 Museo di San Marco

6 Opificio delle Pietre Dure

7 Palazzo Medici Riccardi

8 Piazza della Santissima Annunziata

9 San Lorenzo

Pedestrian precinct

cathedral, was also never completed, nor was the stunningly beautiful marble group, the *Pietà of Palestrina.* One work overshadows the rest, however; standing on an impressive marble plinth in the centre of a circular chamber is the 4.10-m-high (4.48yd) statue of *David*, hewn from a single block of white Carrara marble. Michelangelo's most famous work was moved from its original location in front of the Palazzo Vecchio for safety reasons. The gallery, founded in 1784, also shows works by Italian artists of the 13th to 15th centuries as well as the largest European collection of late Gothic paintings. *Tue–Sun 8.15am–6.50pm | Admission: 6.50 euros, special exhibitions: 10 euros | Advance booking, Tel. 0 55 29 48 83 (supplementary charge: 4 euros) | Via Ricasoli 60*

4 MUSEO ARCHEOLOGICO
(123 F1–2) (Ø G4)

The Archaeological Museum houses the most impressive collection of Etruscan treasures outside the Villa Giulia in Rom and also the second-largest Egyptian collection, after Turin. One of the outstanding pieces represents a mythical creature: the bronze *Chimaere of Arezzo* dating back to around 400 BC. Besides Etruscan and Egyptian objects, there are also prehistoric, Greek and Roman finds on display, for example the famous *François Vase* decorated in the black-figure style with scenes from Greek mythology (600 BC). The beautiful garden contains restored Etruscan tombstones. *Tue–Fri 8.30am–7pm, Sat/Sun until 2pm | Admission: 4 euros | Piazza SS. Annunziata 9b*

5 MUSEO DI SAN MARCO
(126 A5) (*ΩΩ G3*)

When Cosimo I endowed the monks of San Domenico in Fiesole with a monastery in the city in 1435, they gave their fellow Dominican, Fra Angelico, the task of decorating it. The colourful frescos with which the monk filled the cells, the refectory and even the monastery corridors over a period of ten years (1435–45) earned him the name *Beato* ('the blessed one') even during his lifetime. Fra Angelico's large fresco in the Chapter House showing the *Crucifixion,* a *Last Supper* fresco by Domenico Ghirlandaio in the small refectory and, at the head of the staircase to the cell tract, Fra Angelico's most famous work, *The Annunciation,* are highly deserving of a closer look.

Each of the 43 cells was adorned with a fresco by Fra Angelico or one of his assistants. Cells 12 to 14, which were for the Prior's use, now serve as a memorial to Girolamo Savonarola. Cosimo de' Medici often retreated to the double cell 38/39 for extended periods of meditation. Also on the upper floor, the well proportioned *library* by Michelozzo (1444) contains 115 precious codices, miniatures, manuscripts and an illuminated prayer book by Fra Angelico. *Mon–Fri 8.15am–1.50pm, Sat/Sun until 4.50pm, closed 1st, 3rd and 5th Sun as well as 2nd and 4th Mon in the month | Admission: 4 euros | Piazza San Marco 1*

6 OPIFICIO DELLE PIETRE DURE
(123 D1) (*ΩΩ G4*)

In this world-famous academy for resto-ration work, craftsmen still fashion the mosaics out of semi-precious stones and marble for which Florence has been famous since the Renaissance. The finest examples of this *pietra dure* technique are to be seen in the *Cappella dei Principi* in San Lorenzo. Here at the academy, the original designs and a model of the chapel as well as countless other works are on display. INSIDER TIP You can even watch the artisans at work. *Mon–Sat*

Arcades in the inner courtyard of the Palazzo Medici Riccardi

8.15am–2pm, Thu until 7pm | Admission: 4 euros | Via degli Alfani 78 | www.opificio delle pietredure.it

7 PALAZZO MEDICI RICCARDI
(122 C2) (*ΩΩ F4*)

Cosimo the Elder lived here with his family until his death in 1464. Twenty years previously he had engaged Michelozzo to build this prestigious palace which has a grand, rusticated façade. The inner courtyard and arcades, crowned by the Medici coat of arms, were a particular innovation. The *Cappella dei Magi,* decorated by Benozzo Gozzoli in 1459 with delightful landscape frescos, and a few of the rooms on the 1st floor are open to the public. The other rooms house the provincial administration of Florence. *Thu–Tue 9am–7pm | Admission: 7 euros | Via Cavour 1 | www.palazzo-medici.it*

8 PIAZZA DELLA SANTISSIMA ANNUNZIATA (123 E1) (*🗺 G4*)

This harmonious square, featuring an equestrian statue of Ferdinand I by Giambologna and a whimsical fountain by Pietro Tacca, is surrounded on three sides by elegant porticos. To the north is the entrance to the Santissima Annunziata church; to the west the colonnaded walkway in front of the Spedale degli Innocenti, built by Filippo Brunelleschi in 1419 on behalf of the silk merchants. Opposite this is Antonio da Sangallo's *loggia.*
The *Chiesa della Santissima Annunziata* was built in 1250. Legend has it that, one night in 1252, an angel completed an

unfinished fresco showing the 'Annunciation'. The church became a place of pilgrimage. The cloisters show paintings by il Rosso Fiorentino, Jacopo Pontormo and Andrea del Sarto and the frescos by Andrea del Castagno and Perugino in the side chapels are worth a closer look. A representation of the Virgin Mary with supposedly miraculous powers is kept in the chapel immediately to the left of the nave. It is only displayed on 25 March. *Daily 7.30am–12.30pm and 4pm–6.30pm*
From 1445, Brunelleschi's *Spedale degli Innocenti* (orphanage) took in unwanted children who were left in a revolving cabinet to the side of the loggia – even as late as 1875! Andrea della Robbia's terracotta medallions of babies in swaddling clothes decorate the façade of the building, which now contains the *MUDI – Museo degli Innocenti,* home to a fine collection of paintings and frescos from the 14th to 19th centuries. *Daily 10am–5pm | Admission: 5 euros | www.istitutodeglinnocenti.it*

9 SAN LORENZO ⭐ (122 C2) (*🗺 F4*)

There is not one single stone in this church which is not linked in some way to a member of the Medici family. Giovanni

KEEP FIT

Its proximity to the sea is to blame for the fact that there are only two sizeable swimming pools in Florence: the biggest is the *Costoli* (p. 96) and the other, somewhat quieter one, the *Bellariva* (p. 96). If you want to go for a jog, take the bus (12, 13, 17 and 18) to the Parco delle *Cascine:* the over 3 km (1.86mi) of pathways along the Arno are ideal for running, while the rollerbladers get together on the asphalted avenues which

criss-cross the 118-ha (1mi²) park. Sight jogging is the latest trend, combining fitness with taking in the sights. To do this, you can get yourself a personal trainer for 30–70 euros per person – depending on the route and how long you want to go for, e.g. at the *Hotel River* **(130 B3)** (*🗺 H6*)*(Tel. 05 52 34 35 29 | www.hotelriver.com)* or Hotel Lido **(131 D3)** (*🗺 J6*) (*Tel. 0 55 67 78 64 | www.hotel-lido.com).*

di Bicci de' Medici, patriarch of the dynasty, commissioned Brunelleschi in around 1420 with the extension of an Early Christian place of worship, consecrated in the name of St Lawrence back in 393 AD. First of all, Brunelleschi completed the *Sagrestia Vecchia* (Old Sacristy) in 1428,

descendants Giuliano, Duke of Nemours, as well as Lorenzo, Duke of Urbino – each of them the work of Michelangelo. At the beginning of the 17th century, the construction of the *Cappella dei Principi* (Chapel of the Princes), its interior entirely adorned with semiprecious stones,

Adorned with semiprecious stones: Cappella dei Principi in San Lorenzo

the first central-plan building of the Renaissance. Cosimo the Elder, Giovanni's son, continued with construction of the church after his death until its completion in 1446. He lies buried in the crypt. A colourful, round stone slab in front of the main altar indicates the position of the grave. Donatello also found his last resting place alongside his friend and sponsor, Cosimo il Vecchio.

Pope Leo X, Cosimo's great-grandson, made a decisive contribution to the ultimate transformation of the church complex into a giant mausoleum, the INSIDER TIP *Cappelle Medicee*, when he engaged Michelangelo to build the *Sagrestia Nuova* (New Sacristy). It contains the remarkable tombs of Lorenzo il Magnifico, his brother Giuliano and their

marked the climax of the veneration of the ruling family. The designs originate from the son of Cosimo I, Giovanni de' Medici, himself a painter and architect. A door on the left of the church leads to the cloisters and the *Biblioteca Laurenziana*. Tenders were invited for the design of the original rough-cut stone façade we still see today, and plans by Michelangelo do actually exist but were never realised. *Church: Mon–Sat 10am–5.30pm, March–Oct also Sun 1.30pm–5.30pm | Admission: 3.50 euros; Cappelle Medicee: mid-March–Oct daily 8.15am–4.50pm, Nov–mid-March daily 8.15am–1.50pm, closed 2nd, 4th Sun and 1st, 3rd and 5th Mon in the month | Admission: 6 euros, special exhibitions: 9 euros | Piazza Madonna degli Aldobrandini*

SANTA MARIA NOVELLA

One of the city's most beautiful churches, with its splendid marble façade, lends a district and the square in front its name: *Santa Maria Novella.*

The district stretches from the main railway station of the same name northwards as far as the *Fortezza da Basso* and westwards to the *Parco delle Cascine* – the only public green space in the city. To the south, it is bordered by the River Arno and the luxury shopping street *Via dei Tornabuoni*. The *Teatro Comunale,* home to a widely acclaimed music festival *Maggio Musicale Fiorentino,* and the majestic palaces on either side of the river are typical of a quarter which does not revolve entirely around tourism.

■1 INSIDER TIP ▶ MUSEO MARINO MARINI (122 B3) (*ß E–F5*)

Since 1988, the former church of San Pancrazio, which dates back to the Early Christian period, has housed the city's first museum dedicated to modern art. Over 200 works by the sculptor, painter and graphic artist Marino Marini (1901–80) from nearby Pistoia are on display in this skilfully converted place of worship, including his trademark representations of horses. *Wed–Sat and Mon 10am–5pm, closed Aug | Admission: 4 euros | Piazza di S. Pancrazio (Via della Spada) | www. museomarinomarini.it*

■2 MUSEO NAZIONALE ALINARI DELLA FOTOGRAFIA (122 A3) (*ß E4–5*)

Founded by the Alinari brothers in 1852, the *Fondazione Alinari* is the oldest company in the world to specialise in photography and now owns a collection of around 3.5 million pictures. The museum was opened in 2006 and is located in the *Loggia dell'Ospedale di San Paolo* (15th century). The permanent display illustrates the history of photography from its infancy and shows first images. There are

From Bulgari to Versace: a string of luxury labels in the Via dei Tornabuoni

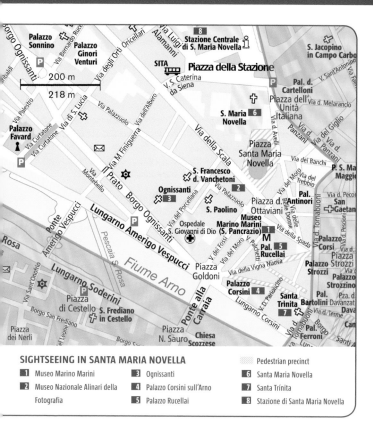

SIGHTSEEING IN SANTA MARIA NOVELLA

1. Museo Marino Marini
2. Museo Nazionale Alinari della Fotografia
3. Ognissanti
4. Palazzo Corsini sull'Arno
5. Palazzo Rucellai
6. Santa Maria Novella
7. Santa Trínita
8. Stazione di Santa Maria Novella

▨ Pedestrian precinct

also special temporary exhibitions. *Thu–Tue 10am–6.30pm | Admission: 9 euros | Piazza Santa Maria Novella 14a/r | www.alinarifondazione.it*

3 OGNISSANTI (125 D6) (*Ø E5*)

The All Saints' Church is a typical example of a sacred building which has been sponsored by a powerful family. The Vespucci's generous patronage not only paid for much of the furnishings and decoration of the church, but the family also founded the adjacent *San Giovanni di Dio* hospital in 1380, which continued in this function until well into the 20th century.

The second church altar on the right features the *Madonna della Misericordia* (an early painting by Ghirlandaio, from around 1473) in which the Virgin Mary spreads her cloak protectively over the members of the Vespucci family. The young man below her right arm is presumed to be the seafarer Amerigo Vespucci, who gave his name to the newly discovered continent of America. In the second chapel of the right transept there is a round stone slab marking the burial place of the great Florentine painter of the early Renaissance, Sandro Botticelli, who was also responsible for the fresco of St Augustine in the monastery refec-

Santa Maria Novella

vases, dominates the Lungarno Corsini. The palace contains the city's largest privately owned art collection, which unfortunately can only be viewed by prior appointment *(Tel. 0 55 21 89 94)*. Every two years in autumn, the *Biennale Internazionale dell'Antiquariato* takes place in the rooms of the palazzo. *Via del Parione 11 | www.bien naleantiquariato.it*

5 PALAZZO RUCELLAI
(122 A–B4) *(ℳ E5)*

Built in 1451, this Renaissance palace belonging to the rich merchant Giovanni Rucellai rates as the most tasteful and elegant in the city. It epitomises the credo of builder and architect Leon Battista Alberti (1402–72) that palatial residences should be beautifully ornamented, elegant and clearly proportioned, rather than ostentatious and imposing. The Rucellai family still live in the palace to this day, which means that the interior is not open to the public. *Via della Vigna Nuova 16*

6 SANTA MARIA NOVELLA
(122 A2) *(ℳ E4)*

In the first story of the *Decameron,* we read of '… seven young ladies (who) assembled in the venerable church of Santa Maria Novella …'. Boccaccio's tale is set during the plague which ravaged 14th-century Florence. The survivors founded numerous chapels in the church to express their gratitude. This first Gothic building in the city was begun in 1246 and finished in 1300. The outer walls are clad in white and green marble, in the style of the Battistero. The upper section of the façade, however, was only completed in 1470 by Leon Battista Alberti thanks to the sponsorship of the Florentine merchant Giovanni Rucellai.

It is worth taking your time to examine

tory. After almost ten years of restoration work, Giotto's famous INSIDER TIP *Crucifix* from the 14th century can once again be marvelled at in the left transept. In the same room, you should also take a look at Ghirlandaio's fresco depicting the *Last Supper* (1480). *Cenacolo del Ghirlandaio | Mon–Sat 7.15am–12.30pm (except Fri) and 4pm–8pm, Sun 9am–1pm and 4pm–8pm | Free admission | Borgo Ognissanti 42*

4 PALAZZO CORSINI SULL'ARNO
(122 A4) *(ℳ E5)*

This imposing Baroque palace, its balustrade crowned with stone statues and the interior, too. The large cycles of frescos give an insight into residential styles and fashions of the 15th century. Among the most beautiful are those by Domenico Ghirlandaio in the choir (1486–90), depicting scenes from the life of the Virgin Mary, the frescos by Filippino Lippi in the *Cappella di Filippo Strozzi* to the right of the main altar and the bleak visions of *The Last Judgement* by Nardo di Cione (around 1357) in the *Cappella Strozzi di Mantova.* In the left of the nave, Masaccio's *Trinity,* painted shortly before his death in 1428, demonstrates a revolutionary awareness and realisation of perspective and proportion. The church also contains works by Brunelleschi (the marble pulpit and a wooden Crucifix in the *Cappella Gondi*, to the left of the main altar), Giotto (Crucifix) and Giovanni della Robbia.

Don't miss the neighbouring *Chiostro verde* (Green Cloister) from 1332, ornamented by Paolo Uccello with images from the Creation story (sadly in poor condition), and the *Cappella Spagnola* (Spanish Chapel) with frescos showing the *Allegory of the Active and Triumphant Church and of the Dominican Order* by Andrea da Firenze. *Church: Mon–Thu 9am– 5.30pm, Fri 11am–5.30pm, Sat 9am–5pm, Sun noon–5pm | Admission: 3.50 euros | Cloisters (entry on the left of the façade): Mon–Thu and Sat 9am–5pm | Admission: 2.70 euros | Piazza S. Maria Novella | www. chiesasantamarianovella.it*

7 INSIDER TIP SANTA TRÍNITA (122 B4) (*M F5*)

Once the most important church in the city, with its origins in the second half of the 11th century, Santa Trínita has among its many art treasures two major works by Domenico Ghirlandaio: the *frescos in the Cappella Sassetti* and the *Adoration of the Magi* from 1485. *Mon–Sat 8am–*

noon and 4pm–6pm, Sun 4pm–6pm | Piazza S. Trínita

8 STAZIONE DI SANTA MARIA NOVELLA (122 A1) (*M E4*)

The main railway station was built by Florentine architect Giovanni Michelucci between 1933 and 1935 and rates as a prime example of Italian Rationalism. Every design detail refers in some way to Florence or to Tuscany: the benches are made of cypress wood, the floor of marble, white from the Apuane Alps, red from Monte Amiata, yellow from Siena and green from the Apennines. Two large frescos by Florentine painter Ottone Rosai grace the bar. *Piazza della Stazione*

SANTA CROCE

Here, too, an entire district takes its name from a church: the Franciscan Santa Croce.

The liveliest quarter in Florence: it's the heart of the city's nightlife, and the many small shops are an invitation to shop till you drop! The bars, restaurants and other eateries around Santa Croce serve up not only the finest the Tuscan kitchen has to offer, but also the whole spectrum of international cuisine.

As far back as Roman times, this quarter was dedicated to entertainment. The 2nd-century *amphitheatre* stood facing the western end of the square – as indicated today by the curvature of the roads around the Piazza de' Peruzzi, Via Bentaccordi and Via Torta. At the southern end of the piazza, below the frescocovered façade of the *Palazzo dell'Antella*, you'll spot a marble disc set into the wall. This marks the halfway line of the 'field' on which *Calcio Storico* is played (see p. 18) – which makes this piazza one of the oldest football pitches in the world!

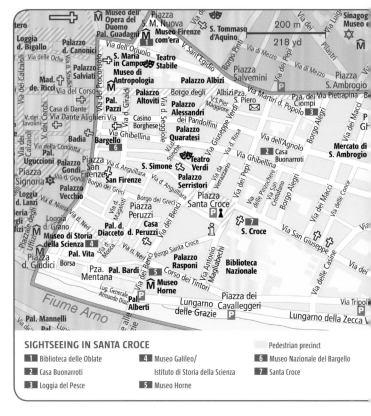

SIGHTSEEING IN SANTA CROCE

1. Biblioteca delle Oblate
2. Casa Buonarroti
3. Loggia del Pesce
4. Museo Galileo/ Istituto di Storia della Scienza
5. Museo Horne
6. Museo Nazionale del Bargello
7. Santa Croce

Pedestrian precinct

■ BIBLIOTECA DELLE OBLATE ※ ●
(123 E3) (𝖒 G5)

The former 14th-century monastery, with its fine cloisters, now houses the municipal library and an extensive media archive (Wed 9am–2pm, Thu/Fri 9am–5pm). On the second of the three floors, there is a large children's section where they can play and leaf through the books (until 6.45pm). It is also possible to read international newspapers free of charge on the INSIDER TIP roof terrace with its sensational view of the dome of the cathedral (so close you feel you could reach out and touch it). Or why

not take a break at the Caffetteria? Mon 2pm–7pm, Tue–Sat 9am–midnight, Via dell'Oriuolo 26 | Tel. 05 52 61 65 12 | www.bibliotecadelleoblate.it

■ CASA BUONARROTI
(123 F4) (𝖒 G6)

This small palazzo was bought by Michelangelo and presented as a gift to the city by a descendent, Cosimo Buonarroti, in 1858. Drawings, plans and mementos of the great artist are on display. Among the early works, are the famous marble reliefs Madonna della Scala (Madonna of the Stairs) and the Battle of the Centaurs. Wed–

Mon 10am–5pm | Admission: 6.50 euros | Via Ghibellina 70 | www.casabuonarroti.it

■3■ LOGGIA DEL PESCE
(130 B2) *(ᗰ H5)*

The loggia was built according to plans by Giorgio Vasari as the fish hall of the old market. Destined for demolition to make way for the Piazza della Repubblica, it was moved at the end of the 19th century to the Piazza dei Ciompi, the venue for today's flea market. *Market: Mon–Sat and last Sun in the month 9am–1pm and 4pm–7pm | Via Pietrapiana*

■4■ INSIDER TIP MUSEO GALILEO/ISTI-TUTO DI STORIA DELLA SCIENZA
(122 C5) *(ᗰ E6)*

The museum is one of the most important of its kind in the world. A large part of it is dedicated to Galileo Galilei. In nine large rooms, mathematic, optical, hydraulic, astronomic and surgical devices are on show, including models of the planets, the first telescope and mercury thermometer and a fine collection of minerals. Don't miss the telescope and lenses the illustrious astronomer used to make his observations and through which he discovered Jupiter's moons, for example. *Wed–Mon 9.30am–6pm, Tue until 1pm | Admission: 8 euros | Piazza dei Giudici 1 | www.museogalileo.it*

■5■ MUSEO HORNE (123 E5) *(ᗰ G6)*

When English art historian and architect Herbert Percy Horne died in 1916, he bequeathed the 15th-century *Palazzo Corsi*, purchased in 1911, to the Italian state. The donation also includes his sizeable art collection of over 6000 works by artists such as Giotto, Simone Martini, Filippo Lippi, Masaccio and Giambologna as well as precious items of furniture from the 14th to 16th centuries. *Mon–Sat 9am–1pm | Admission: 6 euros | Via dei Benci 13 | www.museohorne.it*

■6■ MUSEO NAZIONALE DEL BARGELLO ★ ● (123 D4) *(ᗰ G5)*

Behind the crenellated façade of the Bargello you will find the largest collection of Italian sculptures from the 14th to 16th centuries, the Medici medal collection, significant ivory pieces and majolica from the 15th to 18th centuries, weapons

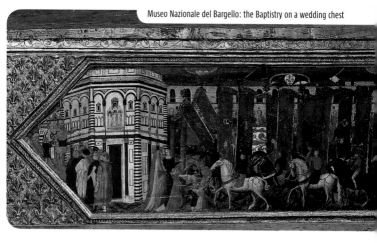

Museo Nazionale del Bargello: the Baptistry on a wedding chest

and small bronze objects. Museum highlights are Michelangelo's *Bacchus* (begun in 1497), the marble bust of *Brutus* (around 1540) and the circular *Tondo Pitti* (1504), which are on show on the ground floor together with works by Cel-

gallows – in use until 1782 – stood next to the fountain in the pretty courtyard decorated with coats of arms. *Tue–Sat as well as 2nd and 4th Sun in the month 8.15am–1.50pm | Admission: 4 euros, special exhibitions: 7 euros | Via del Proconsolo 4*

Santa Croce, built by cathedral architect Arnolfo di Cambio

lini, Giambologna and others. The main room on the upper floor contains Early Renaissance sculptures, including Donatello's *David statues* in marble (1408) and in bronze (1423).

Crowned by a 54-m-high (59yd) tower, the fortress-like palace itself was built in 1254–61 and served as the headquarters of the *Capitano del Popolo* (military governor) and the *podestà (mayor)*. From 1502 to 1859, this was the city prison and residence of the *bargello (captain of police)*, after whom the building is now named. The

7 SANTA CROCE ★
(123 E–F5) (*ØØ G5*)

Santa Croce is the main Franciscan church in Florence. Shortly after his death in 1226, followers of St Francis erected a small chapel here. Soon it was no longer able to accommodate the number of worshipers, so that the foundation stone for this mighty Gothic building was laid in 1294. This was completed in 1385, and a neo-Gothic façade added in 1853. Built in the form of the Egyptian Cross, the basilica is 115 m (125yd) long, the nave 38m (42yd) wide and the transept 73 m (80yd) wide. Consequently, Santa Croce was larger than the church of the rival Dominican Order, Santa Maria Novella, which had been completed shortly before.

The interior features an open, painted trussed roof and straight choir screen, typical of the unpretentious architecture of the mendicant orders. This large place of worship is also known as the 'Pantheon of Florence': 278 *memorial slabs* from the 14th to 19th centuries are set into the floor. Galileo, Michelangelo, Machiavelli, Ghiberti, the composer Rossini and many others are commemorated here with magnificently crafted tombs. Italy's supreme poet, Dante, who died in exile in Ravenna, is also remembered here with a memorial created 500 years after his death. Between 1316 and 1330, Giotto decorated the *funerary chapels of the Bardi and Peruzzi* to the right of the main altar. These frescos are considered to be among the finest of the period. The murals by Taddeo and Agnolo Gaddi in the other chapels are also outstanding. The magnificent *marble pulpit* is by Benedetto da Maiano and the *Annunciation,* fashioned from gilded grey sandstone, (behind the fifth pillar on the right) is a one of Donatello's principle works (1435). To the right of the church is the entrance to the cloistered courtyards with the *Cappella dei Pazzi* and the *Museo dell'Opera di Santa Croce.* The architecture of the Capella dei Pazzi is notable for its clear forms in white and grey and was probably built by Brunelleschi (1429–44). The glazed terracotta *medallions* are the work of Luca della Robbia. The church museum contains Florentine religious art. *Mon–Sat 9.30am–5.30pm, Sun 1pm–5.30pm | Admission: 5 euros | Piazza S. Croce | www.santacroce.firenze.it*

OLTRARNO

There are plenty of ways to discover the district of craftsmen, Oltrarno (beyond the Arno) – ideally, of course, on foot!

You can still sense the 'old' Florence here. The charm of the many hidden workshops is quite unique – where skilled artisans practise their crafts following centuries-old techniques and 'tricks of the trade' to transform leather, glass, bronze, marble, straw, gold or silver – and nowhere else in the city is this atmosphere so authentic. It is usually possible to get a glimpse through open doorways of the craftsmen at work.

Twisting alleyways lead to tiny, enchanting squares where time seems to stand still in the daytime and which, in the evening, become the backdrop for a mass of young revellers thronging the bars and trattorias. Oltrarno also boasts fine Renaissance palaces with famous antique dealers as well as the grandiose *Palazzo Pitti* and the *Boboli Gardens*.

■ FORTE DI BELVEDERE ☆
(129 E4) (*ﾛ F6*)

When Ferdinand I commissioned architect Buontalenti in 1590 with the building of this fortress above Florence, he had the cannons trained on the city: the Medici were never really sure of their hold on authority. Inside the fortress is the elegant, three-storey *Palazzetto di Belvedere.* In the wake of two fatal accidents in 2006 and 2008, in which visitors fell from the perimeter wall, the fortress was closed (hopefully only temporarily). *Via S. Leonardo*

2 GIARDINO DI BOBOLI ⭐ ● 🌿
(129 D–E4) (𝄞 E–F 6–7)

These splendid gardens extend behind the Palazzo Pitti towards the Porta Romana and up to the Forte di Belvedere and feature tree-lined arcades, cypress avenues, fountains and pools, staircases and artificial grottos, an amphitheatre

3 MUSEO STEFANO BARDINI
(130 A4) (𝄞 G6)

The museum bears the name of the renowned merchant, collector, art restorer and photographer Stefano Bardini (1836–1922), who bequeathed his entire collection of antiques to the city upon his death. Following years of renovation

Giardino di Boboli: the former private gardens of the Medici family are now open to the public

and hundreds of marble statues. You should set aside three hours for a stroll around the park (45,000 m²/53,820yd²), savouring the fine views of the city. Chamber music concerts are also held here on summer evenings. *Daily Nov–Feb 8.15am–4.30pm, March until 5.30pm, April/May and Sept/Oct until 6.30pm, June–Aug until 7.30pm, closed 1st and last Mon in the month | Admission: 7 euros, special exhibitions: 10 euros, ticket valid for Giardino di Boboli, Museo degli Argenti, Galleria del Costume, Museo delle Porcellane and Giardino Bardini | Entrances in Palazzo Pitti, Via Romana and Porta Romana | www.giardinodiboboli.it*

work, which was completed in 2009, visitors have been able to marvel at works by artists such as Donatello, Antonio del Pollaiuolo and Tiepolo as well as the original bronze sculpture of the *porcellino* by Pietro Tacca, a replica of which stands in front of the *Loggia del Mercato Nuovo,* much to the delight of thousands of tourists. *Sat–Mon 11am–5pm | Admission: 5 euros | Via dei Renai 37*

4 MUSEO ZOOLOGICO 'LA SPECOLA'
(129 D–E4) (𝄞 E6)

The former observatory, *La Specola,* now houses a zoological collection, which will also fascinate kids. It includes stuffed ani-

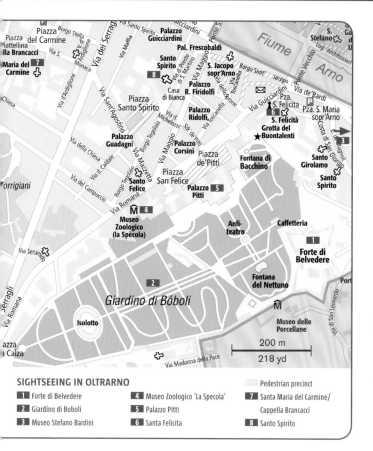

SIGHTSEEING IN OLTRARNO

1 Forte di Belvedere
2 Giardino di Boboli
3 Museo Stefano Bardini
4 Museo Zoologico 'La Specola'
5 Palazzo Pitti
6 Santa Felicita
7 Santa Maria del Carmine/
Cappella Brancacci
8 Santo Spirito

Pedestrian precinct

mals, everything from tarantulas to giant tortoises, plus an interesting display of butterflies. Don't miss the – albeit quirky – INSIDER TIP anatomy department of the museum. It has on show over 1400 at times breathtakingly life-like wax models of human organs and replicas of entire 'skinned' bodies laid out in glass cabinets, some of them bedded on satin. The majority of the anatomical specimens were fashioned by Clemente Susini between 1775 and 1814 in the museum's own wax modelling workshop, and were used originally to teach medical students. *Tue–Sun 9.30am–4.30pm | Admission: 6 euros | Via Romana 17 | www.msn.unifi.it*

5 PALAZZO PITTI ●
(129 E4) *(E–F6)*

The core building of this great palace was built for Florentine merchant Luca Pitti in 1457. Enlarged gradually over the centuries to its current dimensions – the façade is 205 m (224yd) long and 36 m (39yd) high – the palace was home to the grand dukes of Tuscany until 1859.

When Florence was Italy's capital (1865–71), King Victor Emanuel II resided here. Today, the Palazzo Pitti and its adjacent buildings accommodate seven museums and collections. The private painting collection of the grand dukes in the left wing of the palace formed the basis for the *Galleria Palatina* (Palatine Gallery); after the Uffizi, the most important repository of paintings in Florence. The walls of 30 magnificently appointed rooms on the upper floor are literally covered with famous examples of European painting. Highlights of the collection include works by Titian, Raphael, Tintoretto, Giorgione, Rubens, Caravaggio, van Dyck and Velázquez.

On the right-hand side of the upper floor are the *Appartamenti Reali* (Royal Apartments): truly fit for a king. The *Galleria d'Arte Moderna* (Modern Art Gallery) is located on the top floor. In 30 rooms, only some of which are open to the public, the entire spectrum of Tuscan painting of the 18th to 20th centuries is on display. Be sure to take a look at the works of the *Macchiaioli Movement.* So named because of their use of patches or spots of colour ('macchie'), they are regarded as forerunners of the Impressionists.

The *Museo degli Argenti* (Silver Museum) is housed in rooms which were decorated particularly elaborately for the wedding of Ferdinand II and Vittoria della Rovere in 1634. It contains the Medici silver as well as objects in gold, precious stones and ivory. Behind the palace, in the *Giardino di Boboli,* is the *Palazzina della Meridiana,* now the home of the *Galleria del Costume* (Costume Museum). It boasts thousands of items of clothing from the 18th century right down to the creations of the famous designers of the present day.

In the Cavalier's Garden, the Medici grand dukes used to breed silkworms; today the Palazzina del Cavaliere houses the *Museo delle Porcellane* (Porcelain Museum) with a must-see collection of famous-name pieces from the 18th and 19th centuries. *Galleria d'Arte Moderna, Galleria Palatina and Appartamenti Reali: Tue–Sun 8.15am–6.50pm | Admission: 8.50 euros, special exhibitions: 12 euros; Museo degli Argenti, Galleria del Costume, Museo delle Porcellane: daily Nov–Feb 8.15am–4.30pm, March until 5.30pm, April/May and Sept/Oct until 6.30pm, June–Aug until 6.50pm, closed first and last Mon in the month | Admission: 7 euros, special exhibitions: 10 euros | Ticket valid for Giardino di Boboli, Museo degli Argenti, Galleria del Costume, Museo delle Porcellane and Giardino Bardini | Museo delle Carrozze by appointment only, Tel. 05 52 38 86 11 | Piazza Pitti*

6 SANTA FELICITA (122 B6) (*M F6*)

What was probably the first Christian church in Florence stood on this site on the Piazza Santa Felicita, directly behind the Ponte Vecchio. The interior of its successor, rebuilt in 1739 in the high Baroque style, contains two Mannerist gems: the altarpiece showing the *Deposition from the Cross* and the fresco of the *Annunciation* by Pontormo (1525–28). *Mon–Sat 9.30am–12.30pm and 3.30pm–5.30pm | Piazza S. Felicita 3*

7 SANTA MARIA DEL CARMINE/CAPPELLA BRANCACCI (129 D3) (*M E5*)

The fine church with its plain, rough-cut stone façade (under restoration since 2009) can boast a great treasure of Renaissance painting: the frescos in the *Cappella Brancacci* depicting scenes from the life of St Peter. When the original church of the Carmelite Order (from 1268) was almost completely destroyed by fire in 1771, this chapel at the end of the right transept remained untouched by the flames. You can access it today through the courtyard, to the right of the entrance to the church. The 15-part *fresco cycle*, begun in 1423 by Masolino da Panicale and Masaccio, was completed in 1483 by Filippino Lippi. Masaccio's frescos in particular (mostly on the left-hand wall of the chapel) are considered to have paved the way for subsequent artistic developments, due to their inspired depiction of light and shadow and the geometric arrangement of the human figures. Following painstaking restoration work, the frescos have been returned to their original colourful brilliance. *Chapel: Mon and Wed–Sat 10am–5pm, Sun 1pm–5pm | By appointment only, Tel. 05 52 38 21 95 | Admission: 4 euros | Piazza del Carmine 14*

8 SANTO SPIRITO (122 A5–6) (*Ø E6*)
The Augustinians of Santo Spirito settled here in the mid-13th century, and the school they ran here soon became a centre for Humanist studies. The church was built between 1438 and 1482 according to plans by Brunelleschi, and is characterised by its well proportioned, yet una-

dorned façade. The interior, with its 47 grey sandstone columns, impresses with its clear lines, broken only by the Baroque baldachin altar. Don't miss the wooden crucifix by Michelangelo and an altarpiece by Filippino Lippi (1488) in the fifth chapel of the right transept. In the former refectory, the Cenacolo, which is accessed on the left of the church entrance, Andrea Orcagna painted frescos depicting the Last Supper (1360) and the Crucifixion. In front of the church, the many bars and eateries on the INSIDER TIP *Piazza S. Spirito* make it a popular meeting place in Oltrarno. *Mon/Tue, Thu–Sat 10am–12.30pm and 4pm–5.30pm, Sun 4pm–5.30pm | Piazza S. Spirito 29*

OUTSIDE THE CITY

CERTOSA DI FIRENZE (133 D3)
Built in 1314, Florence Charterhouse is an architectural gem; a Carthusian monas-

A number of trattorias line the Piazza Santo Spirito in Oltrarno

tery with cloisters, a library, monk's cells, underground passages and chapels. It's worth a visit just to see Pontormo's Mannerist frescos and the panel paintings in the Pinacoteca by Andrea del Sarto. In return for a donation, Cistercian monks will show visitors around the complex. *Tue–Sat 9am–11am and 5pm–4pm, in summer until 5pm, Sun afternoons only | Bus 37*

FORTEZZA DA BASSO
(125 D–E4) (*∅ E–F3*)

Upon the Medici's return from exile, Duke Alessandro commissioned architect Antonio Sangallo in 1532 with the construction of this massive, star-shaped fortress at the southern end of the city to be better prepared for possible people's revolts. Twice a year it hosts the large international fair for men's fashions, *Pitti Uomo (*trade customers only; *www.pitti mmagine.com), as well as other trade exhibitions, congresses and events. *Viale Filippo Strozzi | Bus 1, 2, 4, 6, 8, 11, 12, 13, 14, 17, 20, 23, 57*

PARCO DELLE CASCINE
(124 A–B5) (*∅ B–C 3–4*)

Covering an area of 1.6 km2, the park is located on a promontory between the rivers Arno and Mugnone. It is the site of the *Ippodromo delle Cascine*, Florence's horse racing track and has a number of bridle paths and various sports facilities. *Piazzale delle Cascine | Bus 12, 13, 17, 18, C3, Tram 1*

INSIDER TIP ▶ PIAZZALE MICHELANGELO
🔍 (130 B4) (*∅ H6*)

This huge observation point is perched high up above the Arno in the south of the city, with café, restaurant, bar and plenty of parking spaces. The fabulous view from here is much loved by residents and tourists alike. A highly conspicuous bronze copy of Michelangelo's *David and the Four Allegories* dominates the square. *Bus 12, 13*

RELAX & ENJOY

Grab yourself a good read and relax in a bar. If this is your idea of an enjoyable, relaxing day, head for somewhere like the *Libreria Edison* (122 C3) (*∅ F5*) *(Mon–Sat 9am–midnight, Sun 10am–midnight | Piazza della Repubblica 27r | www.libreriaedison.it)* or the *Melbookstore* (122 C3) (*∅ F4*) *(Mon–Wed 9am–8pm, Thu–Sat 9am–midnight | Via dei Cerretani 16r | www.melbookstore.it)*.
In the oasis of the *Giardino di Boboli* you can say goodbye to the urban hustle and bustle and stroll past the fountains, statues and grottos, taking an occasional glimpse at the city below.
In the summer, there is nothing more refreshing than sitting over a cocktail at the *Bar Flò* (130 B4) (*∅ H7*) with the most beautiful city in the world at your feet *(7pm–1am | Piazzale Michelangelo 84 | www.flofirenze.com)*. In the winter, a wellness package at the ● *Fonbliù* (129 D5) (*∅ D7*) gets you going again *(Mon–Fri 8.30am–8.30pm, Sat 9am–6pm | Piazzale di Porta Romana 10r | Tel. 05 52 33 53 85 | www.fonbliu.com)*. Enjoy the elegant, luxurious surroundings of ● *SoulSpace*, a spa in an old palazzo, with pool, hammam and great treatments *(10am–8pm | Via S. Egidio 12 | Tel. 05 52 00 17 94 | www.soulspace.it)*.

SAN MINIATO AL MONTE ⭐ ☀
(130 B5) *(ᗰ H7)*

Visible for miles around, this treasure of Romanesque architecture, the church of St Minias on the Mountain, stands on a hill south of the Arno. The view over Florence from the square in front of the church is truly fabulous. A church has stood on this spot since the days of Charlemagne; presumably built to mark the grave of St Minias, who died a martyr in 250 AD. His remains are kept in a shrine in the crypt.

The façade of today's basilica (1018–1207) is clad in encrustations of white Carrara marble and green serpentine. Floor, choir screen and pulpit are ornamented with exquisite marble inlays. Painted in 1297, the apse mosaic showing the *Enthroned Christ* has been restored on many occasions.

The rest of the church interior is no less impressive. At the end of the nave is the freestanding *Cappella del Crocefisso* by Michelozzo (1448), its barrel-vaulted ceiling decorated with rosettes and blue majolica tiles by Luca della Robbia. The altarpieces (around 1396) came from the atelier of Agnolo Gaddi. The left-hand nave contains the *Cappella del Cardinale del Portogallo,* whose tomb was designed by Rossellino; the chapel ceiling with tondi – circular reliefs made of coloured, glazed terracotta – are by Luca della Robbia (1461–66).

Between 1373 and 1552 – and again today – the church and the adjacent *Palazzo dei Vescovi* belonged to the Olivetan Order, a Benedictine Congregation, whose ● vespers chants can be heard in the church every day at around 5.30pm. *Daily 8am–12.30pm and 3pm–5.30pm | Via del Monte alle Croci | Bus 12, 13*

Perched high above the city: San Miniato al Monte

SINAGOGA/MUSEO EBRAICO
(130 B2) *(ᗰ H4–5)*

Building work on the Synagogue in Florence was completed in 1882, and the result is a fine example of neo-Moorish architecture. The interior is decorated entirely with frescos. The mosaics, stained-glass windows and ornamentations in bronze and wood are also worthy of note. The story of the Jews in Florence is documented on the first floor through photographs, paintings and ritual objects. *Oct–March Sun–Thu 10am–3pm, April–Sept Sun–Thu until 6pm, Fri always 10am–2pm, closed Sat and on Jewish holidays | Admission: 5 euros | Via Farini 4/6 | www.firenzebraica.net | Bus 6, 14, 23, 31, 32, C1*

FOOD & DRINK

The Italians love to indulge themselves at the table; they enjoy their food – often dining for hours on end. And it's true; you can eat your fill, even in Florence, without breaking the bank.

Trattorias often have a *menu a prezzo fisso*, i.e. a dish of the day at a fixed price. Self-service restaurants may be cheaper, but are generally not to be recommended as they only serve very boring, run-of-the-mill food. Depending on your taste, you can also get a bite to eat at one of the many bars, *wine bars* and *enoteche* which serve some quite sophisticated speciality dishes and menus from lunchtime onwards. There is a large selection of wines and the ambience is relaxed.

If you prefer to eat in more elegant surroundings and savour some famous, good Tuscan cooking, you should visit a *ristorante* or at least a *trattoria*. Normally the kitchens are open between 12.30pm and 2.30pm and from 7.30pm to 10.30pm. In the evenings, it is advisable to book a table in advance. Many restaurants are closed in August, when most Florentines are on holiday, and also between Christmas and the New Year. (See individual entries for details of special closing times, if known.)

The atmosphere in a *trattoria*, occasionally also known as an *osteria*, is informal; here, you can choose one of the *specialità della casa* (specialities of the house) and drink a *vino della casa* (house wine) to go with it. Even an absolutely top-class restaurant can call itself a *trattoria*: you just have to take a look outside at

More than pizza and pasta – in Florentine restaurants, what counts are fresh ingredients and the Tuscan culinary tradition

the prices and the list of accepted credit cards to clear away any doubts you may have had.

A charge per person for *pane e coperto* (bread and cover charge) is almost always added to the actual price of the meal; this varies between 1 euro and 5 euros. On top of this there is often a supplementary service charge of 10–16 per cent. Tipping is customary (ten per cent). Wait until you have received your change, then leave *il resto*, the rest, on the table when you leave.

Tuscan cuisine is steeped in tradition and is dictated by whichever ingredients are in season at the time. Freshness and authenticity of flavours are particularly important. Stodgy sauces and indefinable side dishes are frowned upon and condemned as superfluous culinary fashion trends. Meat is generally grilled, and vegetables gently steamed and refined with a dash of olive oil. Remember that vegetable side dishes, the *contorni*, must be ordered separately.

Generally speaking, the restaurant menu

See and be seen: Caffè Gilli on the Piazza della Repubblica

looks something like this: *antipasto* (starter), *primo piatto* (first course), *secondo piatto* (main course), *contorno* (side dish), *dolce* (dessert) or *formaggio* (cheese) and *caffè* (espresso). You should round off your meal with a *digestivo* or a glass of *vin santo*.

A word of warning: In the city centre, prices in bars and cafés are often doubled if you sit down rather than remain standing at the bar to enjoy your coffee and *brioche*.

CAFÉS

CAFFÈ FLORIAN (122 B4) (*⌀ F5*)

A little smaller than the original perhaps, but this branch of the famous Caffè Florian in Venice has lots of class. *Sept–June Mon–Fri 8.30am–8pm, Sat 9am–8.30pm, Sun 9.30am–7.30pm | Via del Parione 28r | www.caffeflorian.com*

CAFFÈ PITTI (122 A6) (*⌀ E6*)

Opposite the Palazzo Pitti, with Art-Deco furnishings, sofas and good pastries. Between noon and 3pm there's also a 3-course menu for 15 euros. *Daily 11am–*midnight; in winter: Tue–Sun | Piazza Pitti 9 | www.caffepitti.it*

GILLI (122 C4) (*⌀ F5*)

Founded in 1733 and still immensely popular, especially thanks to its excellent cakes. Elegant ambience and historical charm. *Wed–Mon 7.30am–1am | Via Roma 1 | www.gilli.it*

GIUBBE ROSSE (122 C4) (*⌀ F5*)

Bar and nostalgic café. Around 1900, this was the daily haunt of the literary and artistic crowd. The waiters in their red waistcoats *(giubbe rosse)* also serve whole menus. *Thu–Tue 7.30am–1.30am | Piazza della Repubblica 13r | www.giubbe rosse.it*

RIVOIRE ● (122 C4) (*⌀ F5*)

Expensive (if you sit down at a table), but in a class of its own. Don't leave town without trying a **INSIDER TIP** *cioccolata calda con panna* (hot chocolate with whipped cream); the Rivoire is as much a part of Florence as the Palazzo Vecchio opposite. *Tue–Sun 8am–midnight | Piazza della Signoria 5r | www.rivoire.it*

ICE CREAM PARLOURS

GELATERIA CARABÈ (123 D1) *(ᗰ G4)*
Delicious ice cream creations and *granita*. *Daily 9am–1.30am; in winter: 11am–8pm | Via Ricasoli 60r | www.gelateriacarabe.it*

INSIDER TIP ▶ **GROM** (122 C3) *(ᗰ F5)*
The know-how behind making the ice cream comes from Turin; the ingredients from all over the globe. *April–Oct 10.30am–midnight, Nov–Mar until 11pm | Via del Campanile/corner of Via delle Oche | www.grom.it*

VIVOLI ★ ● (123 E4) *(ᗰ G5)*
Popular gelateria offering no less than forty different flavours. *Tue–Sat 7.30am–midnight, Nov–Mar until 9pm, Sun from 9am | Via Isola delle Stinche 7 | www.vivoli.it*

ENOTECHE & SNACK BARS

LA BOULANGERIE (122 B3) *(ᗰ F4)*
Ideal for a quick bite in between meals: good baguettes, salads and snacks. *Wed– Sun 8am–8pm, Mon/Tue until 5 pm | Via de' Rondinelli 24r | www.ilrifrullo.com*

MAMA'S BAKERY (129 D3) *(ᗰ E6)*
Good American-style sandwiches in a Florentine setting. *Mon–Fri 8am–5pm, Sat 9am–3pm | Via Della Chiesa 34r | Tel. 0 55 21 92 14 | www.mamasbakery.it*

'INO (122 C5) *(ᗰ F5)*
Here, in a tiny side street behind the Piazza della Signoria, you can create a kind of do-it-yourself gourmet sandwich and enjoy a good glass of wine to wash it down. *Daily 11am–5pm | Via dei Georgofili 3r–7r | Tel. 0 55 21 92 08 | www.ino-firenze.com*

INSIDER TIP ▶ **PENSAVO PEGGIO!** (122 A3) *(ᗰ E5)*
It's practically impossible to eat well and cheaply in the centre of Florence – but here's the exception to the rule! Freshly prepared pasta dishes at lunchtime, followed by delicious fish in the evenings. *Mon–Sat | Via del Moro 51r | Tel. 0 55 28 54 86 | www.bacchino.it*

MARCO POLO HIGHLIGHTS

★ **Vivoli**
Try what is probably the best ice cream in town! It won't be easy, though, choosing from the over 40 flavours waiting to attack your taste buds → p. 63

★ **Cantinetta Antinori**
Here, you can not only drink the world-famous wines from the Antinori cellars; there is a selection of tasty dishes to try, too → p. 65

★ **Il Cibreo**
Culinary empire in the market quarter of Sant'Ambrogio → p. 65

★ **Omero**
Popular country inn serving excellent Tuscan specialities with fantastic panoramic views thrown in → p. 65

★ **Beccaio**
Choose your steak from the cool cabinet – and even the cold store is anything but hidden → p. 66

★ **Obikà Mozzarella Bar**
The variety of tasty Mozzarella creations will surprise you → p. 67

★ **Il Santo Bevitore**
Cuisine which skilfully unites tradition and modernity → p. 67

★ **Fiaschetteria Trattoria Mario**
Typical Florentine dishes in a tiny restaurant → p. 69

LOCAL SPECIALITIES

▶ **arista alla fiorentina** – grilled fillet of pork with rosemary and garlic

▶ **baccalà alla fiorentina** – stockfish in tomato sauce with basil

▶ **biscotti di Prato (cantucci)** – almond biscuits to be dipped in vin santo, a sweet dessert wine (photo, top right)

▶ **bistecca alla fiorentina** – a 3.5-cm (1 1/2 in) thick T-bone steak (photo, top left)

▶ **carciofi fritti** – fried quartered artichokes

▶ **cinghiale (coniglio) in umido** – wild boar or rabbit in tomato sauce

▶ **crostini toscani** – toasted bread spread with a paste made of chicken liver, capers and fresh herbs

▶ **fagioli all'uccelletto con salsicce** – white beans in tomato sauce with sage and pork sausages

▶ **fettunta** – toasted slices of white bread: in summer with tomatoes and basil; in winter with garlic and drizzled with freshly pressed olive oil

▶ **lesso (bollito misto) con salsa verde** – boiled meat (beef, tongue, chicken) with green herb sauce

▶ **minestrone/zuppa di verdura** – thick vegetable soup

▶ **panzanella** – a summer salad served on soaked white bread and tomatoes

▶ **pappa al pomodoro** – luke-warm tomato and bread soup

▶ **pollo al mattone** – chicken, pressed flat under a brick and roasted over a wood fire

▶ **ribollita** – re-heated vegetable soup with white beans and bread

▶ **tagliata** – steak, stripped from the bone and cut into strips

▶ **tagliatelle alla lepre (al cinghiale)** – ribbon noodles with hare or wild boar ragout

▶ **trippa alla fiorentina** – calf tripe with tomato sauce

INSIDER TIP PROCACCI (122 B3) (*ØØ F5*)
If your palate calls for a glass of good white wine and an exquisite truffle pâté sandwich, rather than sweet snacks, and if you favour a slightly genteel atmosphere, you'll go crazy for this place! *Mon–Sat 10am–8pm | Via Tornabuoni 64r | www.procacci1885.it*

VIVANDA ☺ (129 D3) (*ØØ E5*)
An enoteca which offers only organic wines – and 120 different ones at that. To go with them, small dishes made from organically produced ingredients. *Daily from lunchtime | Via S. Monaca 7r | Tel. 05 52 38 12 08 | www.vivandafirenze.it*

RESTAURANTS: EXPENSIVE

CAFFÈ CONCERTO ☆ (131 D3) (*K6*)
Fabulous terrace with a view over the Arno; elegant surroundings, agreeable service and excellent international cuisine. *Mon–Sat | Lungarno Cristoforo Colombo 7 | Tel. 0 55 67 73 77 | www.caffe concerto.net*

CANTINETTA ANTINORI ★
(122 B3) (*F5*)
At this pleasant *cantinetta* (wine bar) in the Palazzo Antinori, you can not only sample the famous wines from this wine-growing dynasty, but also try the appetizing foods produced on the Antinori estates. This has long been a favourite meeting place for Florentine movers and shakers. *Mon–Fri | Piazza Antinori 3r (Via Tornabuoni) | Tel. 0 55 29 22 34 | www. cantinetta-antinori.com*

IL CIBREO ★ (130 B2) (*H5*)
Fabio Picchi has found a way of introducing everyone to the finest Tuscan cuisine – without a trace of pasta on the menu. He also relishes the opportunity to present the changing dishes of the day in person. The somewhat cheaper *Cibreino* round the corner is also run by Picchi *(see Restaurants: Moderate)*. Reservation required. *Tue–Sat | Via del Verrochio 8r | Tel. 05 52 34 11 00 | www.cibreo.com*

OMERO ★ ☆ ● (133 E3) (*F8*)
A popular choice with Florentines for its fine regional specialities. You enter the dining room (with its fantastic view of the surrounding countryside) through the *bottega,* where hams and salami hang from the ceiling and you can also get yourself a simple ham sandwich. Galileo Galilei once lived in the palazzo opposite. *Wed–Mon | Via Pian dei Giullari 11r | Tel. 0 55 22 00 53 | www.ristoranteomero.it*

TAVERNA DEL BRONZINO
(126 A5) (*G3*)
Elegant restaurant serving the best the Tuscan kitchen can offer and featuring a particularly well-stocked wine cellar *(book in advance). Mon–Sat | Via delle Ruote 27r | Tel. 0 55 49 52 20*

Il Cibreo is a Florentine institution and renowned for its epicurean delights

RESTAURANTS: MODERATE

RESTAURANTS: MODERATE

4 LEONI (122 B6) *(⚏ F6)*
Trademark trattoria in which you can enjoy very good home-made pasta and savour the famous T-bone steak, the *bistecca alla fiorentina*! *Closed Wed lunchtime | Via de' Vellutini 1/corner of Via Toscanella | Tel. 0 55 2185 62 | www.4leoni.com*

BECCAIO ⭐ (131 D4) *(⚏ J6)*
Vegetarians beware: Here, you can look through a glass partition into the cold store and you can select your desired cut of meat from the cool cabinet! *Mon–Sat evenings only, Sun also lunchtime; closed mid-Aug | Lungarno Ferrucci 9c/r | Tel. 05 56 58 72 28 | www.beccaio.com*

LA BOTTEGA DI ROSA (122 B3) *(⚏ F5)*
Dine in the company of the business fraternity and Florentine families. *Daily | Via del Campidoglio 8/14rm | Tel. 05 52 67 04 23 | www.labottegadirosa.it*

CAVOLO NERO (129 D3) *(⚏ E6)*
A relative newcomer on the restaurant scene, with a garden, in a street to the south of the Arno. Fish dishes are a speciality. *Mon–Sat, evenings only | Via dell'Ardiglione 22 | Tel. 0 55 29 47 44 | www.cavolonero.it*

INSIDER TIP COCO LEZZONE
(122 B4) *(⚏ E5)*
For years now, one of the places to be. Florentine society people squeeze into the cramped interior to enjoy superlative cuisine. *Closed Sun and Tue evenings | Via del Parioncino 26r | Tel. 0 55 28 71 78*

IL GUSCIO (128 C3) *(⚏ D5)*
Typical trattoria, offering good cooking and a long wine list. *Tue–Sat evenings only | Via dell'Orto 49/A | Tel. 0 55 22 44 21 | www.il-guscio.it*

LUNGARNO 23 (123 D6) *(⚏ G6)*
Everything from the Chianina breed of cow: carpaccio, roast beef, steak

GOURMET RESTAURANTS

Enoteca Pinchiorri (130 A2) *(⚏ G5)*
One of the finest restaurants in Italy! Great cuisine and superb wines in truly fabulous surroundings. From 90 euros. *Tue–Thu evenings only, Fri/Sat lunchtime and evenings | Via Ghibellina 87 | Tel. 0 55 24 27 77 | www.enotecapinchiorri.com*

Onice (130 C5) *(⚏ H6–7)*
Gourmet restaurant with 🔆 view over Florence; regional specialities with a touch of the Orient. From 70 euros. *Daily | Hotel Villa La Vedetta | Viale Michelangelo 78 | Tel. 0 55 68 16 31 | www.villalavedettahotel.com*

Relais le Jardin (130 B1) *(⚏ H4)*
Intimate restaurant, praised to the skies by every gourmet guide in Italy. In summer you can eat in the enchanting garden. From 70 euros. *Mon–Sat | Hotel Regency | Piazza d'Azeglio 3 | Tel. 0 55 24 52 47 | www.regency-hotel.com*

Ristorante Villa San Michele (U E2)
Every meal is an experience, when enjoyed under the loggia of this luxury hotel in the former monastery. And there's an 🔆 amazing view over the city. From 90 euros. *Mid-Mar–mid-Nov daily | Fiesole | Via Doccia 4 | Tel. 05 55 67 82 00 | www.villasanmichele.com*

tartare and exquisite hamburgers. *Mon–Sat | Lungarno Torrigiani 23 | Tel. 05 52 34 59 57 | www.lungarno23.it*

INSIDER TIP DA MIMMO
(125 F5) (*ω G3*)

Mimmo is committed to using only fresh ingredients for his excellent dishes – one more reason to come for a meal to this beautiful 17th-century theatre! *Closed Sat lunchtime and Sun | Via S. Gallo 57–59r | Tel. 0 55 48 10 30 | www. ristorantedamimmo.it*

OBIKÀ MOZZARELLA BAR ★
(122 B3) (*ω F5*)

Since 2009, the elegant Palazzo Tornabuoni has been the place to eat the best Mozzarella in town. If you would like to find out more about Southern Italian cheese making, you can also take part in a cheese-tasting session. *Daily 8am–11pm | Via dei Tornabuoni 16 | Tel. 05 52 77 35 01 | www.obika.it*

OSTARIA DEI CENTOPOVERI
(122 A3) (*ω E4*)

They say Donato Cofano is one of the best chefs in Florence. See for yourself – and be sure to try one of the desserts! *Wed–Mon | Via Palazzuolo 31r | Tel. 0 55 21 88 46 | www.icentopoveri.it*

OSTERIA DE' BENCI (123 E5) (*ω G5*)

Florentine cooking in a welcoming ambience, close to the Piazza S. Croce. *Mon–Sat | Via de' Benci 13r | Tel. 05 52 34 49 23 | www.osteriadeibenci.it*

INSIDER TIP OSTERIA DEI PAZZI
(123 E4) (*ω G5*)

Let Paolo spoil you with a few Florentine delicacies, including the typical *bistecca alla fiorentina*! *Tue–Sun | Via dei Lavatoi 3r | Tel. 05 52 34 48 80*

RISTORANTE DEL FAGIOLI
(123 E5) (*ω G6*)

Unpretentious, old trattoria serving up traditional dishes, such as *bollito misto* (boiled meat), *lingua* (tongue) or *trippa* (tripe). *Mon–Fri | Corso Tintori 47 | Tel. 0 55 24 42 85*

Sweet temptation – the dessert at the Ristorante Villa San Michel

IL SANTO BEVITORE ★
(129 D3) (*ω E5*)

Don't leave without trying a plate of starters, including various types of ham and marinated or grilled vegetables. And to follow, choose the *tartara of* Chianina beef or one of the good fish dishes. Excellent value for money. *Daily except Sun lunchtime | Via S. Spirito 66r | Tel. 0 55 21 12 64 | www.ilsantobevitore.com*

Traditional surroundings and good regional fare: Sostanza detto 'Il Troia'

SOSTANZA DETTO 'IL TROIA'
(122 A3) (📖 E5)

Chagall was among those who came to this trattoria, founded in 1869, to savour its Tuscan specialities. *Mon–Fri, April, May, Sept, Oct also Sat | Via del Porcellana 25r | Tel. 0 55 21 26 91*

AL TRANVAI!
(128 C3) (📖 D6)

When the food tastes as good as it does here, you won't mind squeezing in between the other guests on the wooden benches of this eatery! *Tue–Sat, Mon evenings only | Piazza Tasso 14r | Tel. 0 55 22 51 97 | www.altranvai.it*

TRATTORIA DEL CARMINE
(129 D3) (📖 E5)

Tuscan food, reasonable prices, friendly service. *Mon–Sat; in winter: daily | Piazza del Carmine 18r | Tel. 0 55 21 86 01*

TRATTORIA DELL'ORTO
(128 C3) (📖 D5)

Welcoming, bright interior, pleasant service and Tuscan fare. In summer you can also eat outside. *Wed–Mon | Via dell'Orto 35/A | Tel. 0 55 22 41 48 | www.trattoria dellorto.com*

RESTAURANTS: BUDGET

BRAC (123 D5) (📖 G6)

Eat in a bookshop? Why not? The imaginative vegetarian cooking at the Brunch Art Café is a real alternative. *Mon–Sat 11am–midnight, Sun noon–5pm; closed Aug | Via dei Vagellai 18r | Tel. 05 50 94 48 77 | www.libreriabrac.net*

FIASCHETTERIA NUVOLI (122 C3) (📖 F4)

Don't be put off by the size of this tiny cellar diner. This is a great place to have a snack – best of all at lunchtime – in the company of Florentines. *Mon–Sat 8am–9pm | Piazza dell'Olio 15 | Tel. 05 52 39 66 16*

GOZZI SERGIO (122 C2) (📖 F4)

Behind the market stalls of San Lorenzo, authentic trattoria which has been serving up the same simple fare for decades – and the prices haven't changed much either. *Mon–Sat lunchtime only | Piazza S. Lorenzo 8r | Tel. 0 55 28 19 41*

HOSTERIA DA GANINO (123 D4) *(Ø F5)*
A trattoria of yesteryear: traditional cooking, no-frills service and oh so cosy! *Mon–Sat | Piazza dei Cimatori 4r | Tel. 055214125*

INSIDER TIP ▶ NERBONE (122 B–C1) *(Ø F4)*
The Florentine clientele have been descending at lunchtime on this Mercato Centrale stand since 1872. Typical dishes at reasonable prices. *Mon–Sat 7am–2pm | Mercato Centrale | Via dell'Ariento*

OSTERIA-PIZZERIA BALDOVINO (130 B3) *(Ø G5)*
Value-for-money eatery near Santa Croce. *Via S. Giuseppe 22r | Tel. 0552417 73*

OSTERIA SAN NICCOLÒ (130 A4) *(Ø G6)*
Good Florentine cooking which won't break the bank – till midnight, too. *Mon–Sat | Via S. Niccolò 60r | Tel. 0552342836*

ROSE'S (122 B4) *(Ø F5)*
Trendy. A good place for a light lunch. *Mon–Sat noon–1.30am | Via del Parione 26r | www.roses.it*

PIZZAMAN (U F5)
The best pizza in town: *caprese con bufala.* It's well worth making your way out to one of these restaurants which are a little off the beaten track! *Tue–Sun | Via R. Tedalda 411 (Ø O5) | Tel. 0556917 56; daily | Via del Sansovino 191* (124 A6) *(Ø B4) | Tel. 0557127 38 | www.pizzaman.it*

TRATTORIA CASALINGA (129 E3) *(Ø E6)*
Always full, always good, always the place to be. Very modest trattoria, dishing up traditional Tuscan fare. Book in advance! *Mon–Sat | Via de' Michelozzi 9r | Tel. 0552186 24 | www.trattoriacasalinga.it*

FIASCHETTERIA TRATTORIA MARIO ★ (122 A4) *(Ø F4)*
Tiny, typical trattoria near the Mercato Centrale, always full to bursting. Small selection of local dishes. *Mon–Sat lunchtime only; closed Aug | Via Rosina 2r | Tel. 0552185 50 | www.trattoriamario.com*

TRATTORIA SANT'AGOSTINO (129 D3) *(Ø E6)*
Popular Oltrarno trattoria. You can get a full lunchtime menu, including dessert, for only 13 euros. *Tue–Sun | Via S. Agostino 23r | Tel. 0552102 08 | www.sa23.it*

IL VEGETARIANO (125 F5) *(Ø G3)*
Vegetarian trattoria: small, good quality and value for money. *Tue–Sun, Sat/Sun lunchtime only; closed Aug | Via delle Ruote 30r | Tel. 0554750 30 | www.il-vegetariano.it*

LOW BUDGET

▶ A tasty roll *(panino)* will take care of those hunger pangs between meals, e.g. at the *Pizzicheria Guadagni* **(123 E4)** *(Ø G5) | Mon–Sat 8am–8pm; closed Aug | Via Isola delle Stinche 4r* or in the *Osteria de l'Ortolano* **(123 D1)** *(Ø G4) | Mon–Fri 10am–8pm, Sat until 2pm; closed Aug | Via degli Alfani 91/93r. I Fratellini* **(122 C4)** *(Ø F5)* is also famous for its *panini,* which you eat standing in the street *(Mon–Sat | Via dei Cimatori 38r).*

▶ Cooked offal is one of the more unusual specialities of the Tuscan kitchen: Give the *trippa* a try from one of the value-for-money stands on the *Piazza dei Cimatori* **(123 D4)** *(Ø E5)* or next to the *Loggia del Mercato Nuovo* **(122 C4)** *(Ø F5)* in *Via Calimaruzza!*

SHOPPING

CITY **WHERE TO START?**

Piazza della Repubblica (122 C3–4) *(𝄐 F5)*: Shopping hub in the city: If you want to see the latest from the world of haute couture, keep tight hold of your purse and stroll over to Via Tornabuoni: Armani, Bulgari, Cavalli … The ABC of fashion spelled out on 300 m (330 yd). If that's beyond your means, take a walk along the narrow streets in the opposite direction, where there's something for every budget. Electric minibus C1 and C2, bus 6 and 22; car parking: Stazione Santa Maria Novella.

A dose of retail therapy in Florence is an aesthetic pleasure – but it could also be an expensive one.

Fashion is definitely the absolute top tip when it comes to shopping, especially during the sales *(saldi)* in January/February and in July/August. Pay attention, though; Italian clothing sizes can be confusing to say the least. As a very rough guide, Italian size 42 is equivalent to UK size 10/US size 8. Are you into gold, silver, precious stones or cutlery? If so, head for the area around the Ponte Vecchio, where you'll find not only the real thing, but also imaginative fashion jewellery. Crossing the Arno, you enter the district of Oltrarno, which kicks off with the ● Borgo San Jacopo and its extravagant boutiques, while the territory of the antique dealers extends between

Photo: Jeweller's shops on the Ponte Vecchio

From exquisite boutiques to rustic markets – Florence has something unique for every budget and taste!

Via Maggio, Via Santo Spirito and Borgo San Frediano.

Normal opening hours are Mon–Sat 9am–1pm and 3.30pm–7.30pm. The shops in the city centre do not usually close for lunch; some are even open on Sundays. Food shops are closed on Wednesday afternoons; all other types of shop on Monday mornings. In July/August, many shops close on Saturday afternoons – except fashion boutiques and department stores. Some shops close altogether for two weeks in mid-August, as nearly every Florentine is on holiday.

ANTIQUES

In the district of Santa Maria Novella, there is a string of antique dealers along Via dei Fossi and Borgo Ognissanti, as is the case on the other side of the river around Via Maggio.

ATELIER MELISSA GENTILE
(122 A3) (*ü E5*)

A number of shops are grouped around the pretty inner courtyard of the Palazzo Fossombroni. *Closed Sat | Via dei Fossi 7b/r*

Parmigiano, mortadella or salami: regional specialities from Perini

CASA WOLF (129 D1) (*ⓂⓂ E5*)

Over many years, Renato, a surgeon, collected items of furniture and fabrics. Today, these antiques are up for sale. *Borgo San Frediano 151r | www.casawolf.it*

BOOKSHOPS

GOZZINI (123 D1) (*ⓂⓂ F4*)

A small, well-kept antiquarian bookshop has rarities and bags of atmosphere to offer. *Via Ricasol 49 | www.gozzini.com*

FELTRINELLI INTERNATIONAL (122 C2) (*ⓂⓂ F4*)

Huge selection of foreign-language literature and magazines. *Via Cavour 13 | www.lafeltrinelli.it*

DELICATESSEN

AMARÙ (122 A4–5) (*ⓂⓂ E5*)

Small delicatessen in the style of an old-fashioned grocer's shop. Here, alongside edible Italian specialities, you'll find kitchen utensils. *Piazza Nazario Sauro 14r | www.amarufirenze.it*

LA BOTTEGA DELL'OLIO (122 B5) (*ⓂⓂ F5*)

The finest olive oils and anything else that can be produced from olives. *Piazza del Limbo 2r (Borgo SS. Apostoli)*

OLIO & CONVIVIUM (122 A5) (*ⓂⓂ E5*)

The old shelves are full of delicious specialities to take home with you: olive oil, honey, pasta sauces, wine and much more besides. Or do you fancy a quick bite to eat for lunch? You can also satisfy that desire in this fine palazzo in Oltrarno. *Via S. Spirito 20 | www.convivium firenze.it*

PEGNA (123 D3) (*ⓂⓂ F5*)

This delicatessen near the cathedral has been in existence since 1860. Today, it is a supermarket bursting with culinary treats. *Via dello Studio 8 | www.pegna.it*

INSIDER TIP PERINI (122 B1) (*ﬧ F4*)
An eldorado in the market hall, offering foods of the highest quality. Have yourself a delicious *panino* made with all your favourite ingredients! *Mercato Centrale | Via dell'Ariento | www.periniitalia.it*

VESTRI (123 E4) (*ﬧ G5*)
The finest chocolate in all shapes and flavours; ice cream, too. *Borgo degli Albizi 11r | www.vestri.it*

ONLY IN FLORENCE

BOTTEGA MONTEBELLO (123 E1) (*ﬧ G4*)
Most of the objects on sale here are made of wood and all of them are connected to Florence in some way or another. Original, attractive gifts. *Via dei Servi 111r*

CARLO SAITTA (130 B2) (*ﬧ H5*)
Hand-made paper, printed with artistic designs. You can even watch the artisan papermakers at work. *Via dell'Agnolo 28r*

LEGATORIA LA CARTA (129 D4) (*ﬧ E6*)
Omero Benvenuti has been working as a book binder since 1967. His bound diaries and photo albums are works of art in their own right. *Via Romana 58r | www.legatorialacarta.com*

LUNGARNO DETAILS (122 B–C5) (*ﬧ F5*)
Design objects, accessories and great ideas for gifts. *Lungarno Acciaiuoli 4*

INSIDER TIP OFFICINA PROFUMO-FARMACEUTICA DI S. MARIA NOVELLA (122 A2) (*ﬧ E4*)
Immediately on entering, you are captivated by the scent of Tuscan herbs. The Dominicans founded a monastery apothecary here in 1221; nowadays, you can purchase perfumes and soaps in these hallowed halls. *Via della Scala 16 | www.smnovella.com*

PAOLO CARANDINI (123 F4) (*ﬧ G5*)
Boxes everywhere; made of leather or vellum; some modern, some traditional. *Borgo Allegri 17*

LE PIETRE NELL'ARTE ★
(123 D3) (*ﬧ G4*)
Since the 16th century, the art of fashioning inlays out of semi-precious stones has been passed down here from father to son. Everything from brooches or jewellery boxes to tabletops! *Via Ricasoli 59r | www.scarpellimosaici.it*

★ **Le Pietre nell'Arte**
Inlaid work, just like in the 16th century → p. 73

★ **Sbigoli Terrecotte**
A world of ceramics → p. 74

★ **Nencioni**
Over two million prints in stock → p. 75

★ **Il Bisonte**
All things great and small in finest leather → p. 76

★ **Mercato Centrale**
Eldorado for the gourmet palate → p. 76

★ **Mercato San Lorenzo**
Clothes and much more besides → p. 77

★ **Antico Setificio Fiorentino**
Silk, hand-woven according to historical patterns → p. 79

★ **Loretta Caponi**
Classy nightwear – for kids, too → p. 79

MARCO POLO HIGHLIGHTS

PINEIDER (122 C4) (*📖 F5*)
Exclusive stationery, diaries and personalised writing paper. *Piazza della Signoria 13r | www.pineidershop.com*

SBIGOLI TERRECOTTE ★
(123 E3) (*📖 G5*)
From painted egg cups or prettily glazed water jugs to enormous hand-crafted terracotta vases from Impruneta – it's all available here. *Via S. Egidio 4r | www. sbigoliterrecotte.it*

LOW BUDGET

▶ The flea markets on the Piazza Santo Spirito **(122 A5–6)** (*📖 E6*) *every second Sunday* or around the large fountains of the Fortezza da Basso **(125 D–E4)** (*📖 E–F3*) on every third Sunday in the month are ideal for bargain-hunting.

▶ The outlets round about Florence are popular destinations: *The Mall* **(133 F4)** focuses on brand names such as *Gucci, Zegna, Tod's, Armani, Ferragamo, Fendi and Valentino (daily 10am– 7pm | Via Europa 8 | Leccio/Reggello | bus trips twice a day for 25 euros/ person | Info: Tel. 05 58 65 77 75 | www. outlet-the-mall.com)*. The Designer Outlet Barberino, 30 km to the north, is laid out like a small village, with over 90 international brands *(Tue–Fri 10am– 8pm, Sat/Sun until 9pm, Dec/Jan and June–Sept also Mon 2pm–8pm | Barberino di Mugello, district of Scopicci | Bus SITA from main railway station/Via S. Caterina da Siena, Mon–Sat 8.30am, 12.35pm, 1.30pm, 2.30pm, Sat/Sun 9.30am, 2pm, 4.30pm (approx. 45 min.) for 12 euros | Tel. 0 55 84 21 61 | www.barberino.designer-outlet.it*

GLASS, PORCELAIN & SILVER

ARMANDO POGGI (122 C3) (*📖 F5*)
Armando Poggi is one of the old established companies which sell everything you need for a beautifully laid table. *Via dei Calzaiuoli 103r and 116r | www.apoggi.com*

BRANDIMARTE (128 C2) (*📖 D5*)
Platters, lamps or beakers made from hand-worked silver. *Viale Ariosto 11 c/r | www.brandimarte.com*

COLTELLERIA BIANDA (122 A4) (*📖 E5*)
Since 1820, the Bianda family has been manufacturing knife blades. The tiny shop has hardly changed at all. *Via della Vigna Nuova 86r*

INSIDER TIP ▶ MOLERIA LOCCHI
(128 C2) (*📖 D5*)
Unique glass and crystal cutter's workshop, which looks back on 200 years of history. Here, individual pieces can be restored or authentically reproduced. *Via Burchiello 10 | www.locchi.com*

RICHARD GINORI (122 B3) (*📖 F4*)
The king of Italian porcelain since 1735, now with a value-for-money sales outlet in Sesto Fiorentino (*Viale Giulio Cesare 19* **(133 D2)** (*📖 D5*)). *Via Rondinelli 7 | www.richardginori1735.com*

DEPARTMENT STORES

COIN (122 C4) (*📖 F5*)
Upmarket department store based on the shop-in-the-shop system. Good hosiery department and large sizes – a rarity in Italy. *Daily 10am–7.30pm | Via dei Calzaiuoli 56r | www.coin.it*

LA RINASCENTE (122 C3–4) (*📖 F5*)
If you go up to the well-stocked household goods department on the 4th

floor, then climb the small flight of stairs on the right, you can enjoy a ● ☼ **INSIDER TIP** fantastic view from the roof terrace across the city – and tuck into a cappuccino and a cake, too. The perfume department also has a great range of brands on offer. *Mon–Sat*

23r | www.kensartgallery.com

NENCIONI ★ (123 D4) (*∅ F5*)
Over 2 million copperplate prints from different periods, showing various motifs – whether maps, vedute, plants or animals. There's sure to be a frame to

On the roof terrace of Rinascente

10am–9pm, Sun 10.30am–8pm | Piazza della Repubblica | www.larinascente.it

go with each print, if you wish. *Via della Condotta 25r*

ART & GALLERIES

GALLERIE IL MAGNIFICO (123 D4) (*∅ G5*)
A good selection of Italian paintings, largely from the 19th century. *Via dell'Acqua 6r*

GALLERIA PANANTI (122 A5) (*∅ E6*)
Gallery owner Piero Pananti also publishes much-coveted art catalogues. *Via Maggio 15 | www.pananti.com*

KEN'S ART GALLERY (130 B4) (*∅ G6*)
Here, you'll find mostly avant-garde works and Arte Povera. *Via San Niccolò*

IL TAMARINO (122 A3) (*∅ E5*)
Limited editions of original etchings. Your own special motif can be made to order. *Via del Moro 46r | www.iltamarino.com*

TETHYS GALLERY (122 A6) (*∅ E6*)
Gallery for contemporary photographic art. *Via Maggio 58r | www.tethysgallery.com*

ZECCHI (123 D3) (*∅ F5*)
Paints for artists and restorers. This is the place to find exactly those materials the Renaissance artists used to use. *Via dello Studio 19r | www.zecchi.it*

Colourful selection at the Mercato Centrale

MARTELLI (123 C5) (*ш F5*)

Hand-made gloves, in all styles and colours. *Via Por Santa Maria 18r | www. martelligloves.it*

NATALINO SARTI (123 D5) (*ш G5*)

Whether clothing, shoes, bags or suit-cases, the leather here is hand-crafted, yet still affordable. *Borgo de´ Greci 16r*

INSIDER TIP SCUOLA DEL CUOIO (123 F5) (*ш G5*)

The world-famous school of leatherwork-ing is located in the rooms of the Santa Croce monastery. Here, you can buy bags, jewellery boxes or purses and have them embossed in gold with your initials. *Via di San Giuseppe 5r | www.scuoladelcuoio. com*

MARKETS

The main weekly market takes place every Tuesday morning in the *Parco delle Cascine (124 B5) (ш B–C 3–4)* and there's a small flea market every day on the *Piazza dei Ciompi (130 B2) (ш H5)*. All other markets sell not only fruit and vegetables, but also many other every-day objects.

MERCATO CENTRALE ★ (122 B–C1) (*ш F4*)

The large market hall, built in 1784, is an eldorado for lovers of fine foods. Check out the mouth-watering stalls full of lo-cal produce and work up an appetite for dinner! *Mon–Sat 7am–2pm; in winter: also Sat 4pm–8pm | Via dell'Ariento*

MERCATO DEL PORCELLINO (122 C4) (*ш F5*)

Leather goods, ties, fabrics and souvenirs in the *Loggia del Mercato Nuovo. Tue–Sat 8am–7pm | Via Por S. Maria*

LEATHER GOODS

IL BISONTE ★ (122 A4) (*ш E5*)

Do you need a new suitcase, handbag or perhaps simply a fine purse or wallet? El-egant luggage, mostly made of naturally tanned cowhide or buffalo hide. *Via del Parione 31r | www.ilbisonte.net*

LILIUM (123 D4) (*ш G5*)

Hand-bound photograph albums, exer-cise books or notebooks. *Via del Procon-solo 77r | www.liliumflorence.it*

MERCATO SAN LORENZO ★ ●
(122 B–C 1–2) (◫ F4)

Fashion items, but also gifts, ceramics and knitwear on this large and very touristy market skirting the church of San Lorenzo and on the adjacent Via dell'Ariento. A stroll across the market is always fun, especially if you're on the lookout for a souvenir to take home with you. *Tue–Sat 8am–7pm | Piazza S. Lorenzo*

INSIDER TIP MERCATO DI SANT'AMBROGIO (130 B2) (◫ H5)

Come here to experience the most authentic market atmosphere in Florence. For one thing, there are hardly any tourists, and the stallholders know their local customers by name, swapping recipes and looking forward to their certain return the next day. *Mon–Sat 7am–2pm, Wed/Thu until 7.30pm | Piazza Ghiberti*

MARBLE

RAFFAELLO ROMANELLI (129 E3) (◫ F5)

Do you fancy your own copy of Michelangelo's sculpture of *David* for the garden? The 1 : 1 marble reproduction is to be had for 140,000 euros. If your budget won't stretch to that, there are more affordable items (from 4 euros) in marble and stone, too. *Lungarno Acciaiuoli 72–78r | www.raffaelloromanelli.com*

FASHION

ALTA ROSA ◔ (125 F5) (◫ G3)

Stylish women's fashions made from fabrics which are produced according to ecologically sound practices. *Via San Gallo 84r | www.altarosa.it*

EMILIO PUCCI (122 B4) (◫ F5)

Headquarters of the Pucci fashion dynasty. The Florentine designer's eccentric fabrics are unmistakable. You should at least take a look at them, even if buying is out of the question! *Via Tornabuoni 20–22r | www.emiliopucci.it*

ERMENEGILDO ZEGNA (122 B4) (◫ E–F5)

Clothing and accessories for the fashion-conscious man. *Piazza Rucellai 4–7r | www.zegna.com*

FLÒ ◔ (122 A3) (◫ E5)

Vintage fashions and accessories plus creations by young designers who believe in sustainability. *Lungarno Corsini 30–34 | www.flo-firenze.org*

MADE TO MEASURE

Treat yourself to the luxury of some bespoke garments or footwear; only here in Florence are these crafts practised to such a professional degree. *Rina Milano* can tailor you an elegant dress *(Lungarno Guicciardini, 7r (122 A5) (◫ E5) | Tel. 05 52 34 39 38 | www.rinissima.it)*; gentlemen should turn to *Antonio Liverano (Via dei Fossi 43r (122 A3) (f E5) | Tel. 05 52 39 64 36 | www.liverano.com)*; young shoe expert *Saskia Wittmer* uses a model of your foot to make the shoe of your dreams *(Via di S. Lucia, 24r (129 D1) (◫ E4) | Tel. 0 55 29 32 91)* and the 'world-famous nose' belonging to *Lorenzo Villoresi* can create the perfume that suits you best *(Via dei Bardi 14 (122 C6) (◫ F6) | Tel. 05 52 34 11 87 | www.lorenzovilloresi.it)*.

JEWELLERY & WATCHES

LUISA VIA ROMA (122 C3) (*□ F5*)
The Florentine fashion temple: exclusive boutique on two floors with the latest designs, not only from Italian labels. *Via Roma 19–21r | www.luisaviaroma.com*

ANDREA PALOMBINI (123 E4) (*□ G5*)
Made-to-measure ladies' blouses and gentlemen's shirts fashioned from the most exquisite materials. If your choice is not a perfect fit, it will be altered and sent on within the following two weeks. *Borgo degli Albizi 84r | www.andreapalombini.com*

PITTI VINTAGE (122 A6) (*□ E6*)
Gear from the 1970s and '80s, also by Italian designers, such as Versace, Fendi, Gucci or Ferragamo. *Sdrucciolo de' Pitti 19r | www.pittivintage.com*

JEWELLERY & WATCHES

APROSIO & CO. (122 A5) (*□ E5*)
Imaginative pieces crafted from Venetian glass beads and crystals in the shape of flowers, animals, coral, fruits … *Via Santo Spirito 11 | www.aprosio.it*

ENRICO VERITÀ (122 C3–4) (*□ F5*)
There are only eight traditional watchmakers left in Italy. In this atelier, you have the feeling you've travelled back in time. Repairs are also carried out. *Via de' Calzaiuoli 122r*

EVEN BIJOUX (123 D4) (*□ F5*)
Hand-crafted jewellery according to old and new designs. *Via Dante Alighieri 8r*

SHOES

MONTI CALZATURE (123 D3) (*□ F4*)
If all you need is a comfortable pair of shoes, Monti is sure to have something for you. Also Birkenstock sandals and Dr. Scholl's products. *Piazza Duomo 27r*

SALVATORE FERRAGAMO (122 B4) (*□ F5*)
The 'King of shoemakers' died in 1960, but his acclaimed brand name lives on. Ladies' shoes, accessories and a shoe museum. *Via Tornabuoni 16r | www.salvatoreferragamo.it*

MEDICI VILLAS

A visit to the most magnificent Medici villas in the suburb of Sesto Fiorentino/Castello **(133 D–E2)** is a must on every tourist itinerary. Bus routes 2 and 28 take you there from the main railway station, Santa Maria Novella, in around 30 minutes. *Villa La Petraia (bus stop Sestese 03)* is one of the most impressive Medici residences, and is surrounded by a beautiful park, designed by Tribolo. Scarcely 100m (110yd) away is Villa *Corsini a Castello*, a typical example of Florentine late Baroque architecture, containing a remarkable collection of antique sculptures *(Sat/Sun 9.30am–1pm | Free admission)*. The next bus stop *(Sestese Leo France)* is ideal for the *Villa Reale di Castello;* you can visit the perfectly preserved, Italian-style park and its fountains, statues and grottos *(Villa La Petraia and Park Villa Reale di Castello: Oct–Mar 8.15am–4.30pm/5.30pm, April, May, Sept until 6.30pm, June, Aug until 7.30pm; closed 2nd and 3rd Mon in the month | Joint ticket: 2 euros).*

Limited wearability and affordability – shoes by Ferragamo

FABRICS

ANTICO SETIFICIO FIORENTINO ★ ● (128 C2) (𝄞 D5)

Alessandro Pucci has rejuvenated an 18th-century silk-weaving mill in the San Frediano district, where he produces and sells fabulous fabrics featuring antique designs. Not what you'd call cheap, but the ultimate in exclusivity! *Via Bartolini 4 | www.anticosetificiofiorentino.com*

CASA DEI TESSUTI (122 C3) (𝄞 F5)

The biggest selection of haute-couture textiles. The models are presented by means of video projector and then specially made up for you. Approximately 2000 different fabrics are permanently in stock. *Via dei Pecori 20–24r | www.casadeitessuti.com*

UNDERWEAR & LINEN

FERRINI (122 C4) (𝄞 F5)

High-quality bed- and table linen, nightwear and much more besides. *Via Calimala 5r | www.ferrinifirenze.it*

LORETTA CAPONI ★ (122 B3) (𝄞 F5)

Loretta began learning embroidery at the age of nine. Today, her atelier and showrooms are located in a 650-m² (780-yd²) Renaissance palace, where she still advises her clients, from Florentine high society and among the crowned heads of Europe. *Piazza Antinori 4r | www.lorettacaponi.com*

WINE

The following dealers have a broad selection of fine Tuscan wines:

ENOTECA ALESSI (122 C3) (𝄞 F5)
Via delle Oche 27r | www.enotecaalessi.com

ENOTECA BONATTI (130 C2) (𝄞 J5)
Via Gioberti 68r | www.enotecabonatti.it

ENOTECA F. MURGIA (122 B3) (𝄞 F4)
Via dei Banchi 55–57r

PITTI GOLA E CANTINA (129 D3) (𝄞 E6)
Piazza Pitti, 16

ENTERTAINMENT

CITY **WHERE TO START?**
Don't bother looking for one specific nightclub district – there isn't one. The narrow streets around Santa Croce **(123 E–F5)** *(Ⱳ G5)* are home to a number of bars and clubs. People meet up here at 7-ish for happy hour, drink an aperitif and satisfy their hunger at generous buffets, usually for a fixed price. Later on in the night, dance till you drop in the clubs and discos. The best dance locations, however, are on the edge of town and can only be reached by car or taxi. Electric minibus C3, bus 23, car parking at Piazza Ghiberti

If a stroll through the streets and alleyways of the nocturnal city centre is not your idea of a good night out – although it's a fascinating experience in itself – Florence has plenty of options for an eventful and varied evening. And that's without having a true entertainment district of its own.

The centre has loads of trendy bars and jazz clubs, whereas most discos are on the periphery. The Florentine theatre scene is particularly lively. The 200 or so performances per year are often guest appearances and represent a good cross-section of Italian theatre in general. Advance ticket sales: *Box Office | Via delle Vecchie Carceri 1 | Tel. 0 55 21 08 04 | www. boxol.it*

Whether bar, disco, open-air concert or a dose of culture at the theatre or opera – Florentine nights are anything but boring

TRENDY BARS & PUBS

ASTOR CAFFÈ (123 D3) (*M F–G4*)
Right by the cathedral, every day from 10am till 3am: breakfast, lunch, aperitif and cocktails. As an exception, happy hour lasts from at least 6pm till 2am! *Piazza Duomo 20r*

THE CHEQUERS PUB (122 A3) (*M E4*)
Old England in Florence. Always full. Proverbial rivers of ale flow through this watering hole, which serves typical pub food plus fish 'n' chips, hot dogs and sandwiches. *Daily 6pm–1.30am; happy hour: 6.30pm–8pm | Via della Scala 7*

DOLCE VITA ★ (129 D2) (*M E5*)
See and be seen: First-rate cocktails are mixed during *happy hour* from 5pm, then the place is packed to the gills until 2am. Disco-bar with small exhibitions and mini-concerts. Outside, too, in summer. *Tue–Sun; mid-Aug: closed for 2 weeks | Piazza del Carmine 6r | www.dolce vitaflorence.com*

Nightcap at Zoe

Via Vittorio Emanuele (126 A3) (Ⓜ F1)). From 9pm | Via Nuova de' Caccini 3/corner of Borgo Pinti | Admission: approx. 8 euros | www.jazzclubfirenze.com

KITSCH 1 ⭐ (130 C2) (Ⓜ G4)
Join the many young Italians (and a few foreign students) at this quirky locality for possibly the most decadent *aperitivo* (until 10pm) in town! *Daily 6.30pm–3am | Viale Gramsci 1–5/corner of Piazza Beccaia | www.kitsch-bar.com*

MOYO (123 E5) (Ⓜ G5)
The agenda at this cult hang-out is as follows: from 8am till 3pm, a chat over breakfast; a little discussion over a light lunch; after the aperitif a bit of flirting till the small hours. *Daily 8am–3am | Via dei Benci 23r | www.moyo.it*

NEGRONI (130 A4) (Ⓜ G6)
Meeting place of Florentine movida: In summer guests gather outside; in winter it's shoulder to shoulder at the bar inside for one of the great long drinks. *Mon–Fri 8pm–2am, Sat/Sun from 7pm | Via dei Renai 17r | www.negronibar.com*

REX CAFFÈ (123 F3) (Ⓜ G5)
Imagine an American bar on an ocean liner in the middle of the city: good combination of colourful cocktails, fresh snacks and, after 10 pm, live music. *Mid-May–mid-Sept daily 5pm–2.30am | Via Fiesolana 23r*

INSIDER TIP ▶ IL RIFRULLO
(130 A4) (Ⓜ G6)
Inside, cosy atmosphere in front of the open fire; outside, romantic roof terrace. Here, you can really have a good time, from the first cappuccino of the day to a glass of good wine or a fruity cocktail late at night. *Daily 7am–1am | Via San Niccolò 55r | www.ilrifrullo.com*

HEMINGWAY (129 D3) (Ⓜ E5)
An absolute *must* for chocolate junkies! They also have good, home-made ice cream, cake (unlike much of what you'll get elsewhere in Florence!), many varieties of tea and coffee, crêpes and other tempting titbits. *Mon–Thu 4.30pm–1am, Fri/Sat until 2am, Sun 3.30pm–1am | Piazza Piattellina 9r | www.hemingway.fi.it*

JAZZ CLUB (123 F3) (Ⓜ G4)
The fans flock to their favourite venue from 9pm, on Tuesdays and Thursdays also for the jam session. From June to September, the whole set-up moves to the park at the *Villa Fabbricotti (Tue–Sat |*

TABASCO ⭐ (122 C4) (*ω F5*)

Cocktail bar for men only near the Piazza della Signoria. Till 4 in the morning, this is the heart of the city's homosexual scene. Thu–Sat also disco until 6am. *Piazza di S. Cecilia 3 | www.tabascogay.eu*

VOLUME (122 A6) (*ω E6*)

Bini's old cabinet-maker's workshop has been transformed into a bar with cult status. Against a 1970s backdrop, you can read, eat excellent crêpes, listen to live music or simply have a drink. *Daily 9.30am–1am | Piazza S. Spirito 5r | www.volume.fi.it*

THE WILLIAM PUB (123 E5) (*ω G6*)

Beer a-plenty here, every day from 6pm: Irish, Scottish, English – the biggest selection of beers in Florence. *Via Magliabechi 9r | www.thewilliam.it*

ZOE (130 A4) (*ω G6*)

Popular watering hole, also good for a quick lunch with the young working population of the district of San Nicolò; it also suits the upper-class student fraternity, who get together here for an aperitif. *Daily 8am–2am | Via dei Renai 13r | www.zoebar.it*

DISCOTHEQUES

Opening times can vary according to the time of year. It might be a good idea to ring up first! Admission prices are usually around 25 euros.

CENTRAL PARK ⭐ (124 C5) (*ω C4*)

Popular open-air disco in summer, with six dance floors at the entrance to the *Parco delle Cascine*. Take a look at the event calendar under *www.centralfirenze.it* to find out what's going on. *Wed–Sat | Via Fosso delle Macinate 2*

DOLCE ZUCCHERO (123 E4) (*ω G5*)

Much-loved disco-pub, especially popular with young tourists and students on the European Erasmus Programme. Separate room for live music. *Australian Beach Bar* also with separate entrance. *Tue–Sun 10.30pm–4am | Via Pandolfini 36r*

⭐ **Dolce Vita**
The cocktails go down well not only during happy hour → p. 81

⭐ **Kitsch 1**
Great aperitifs in a bar that's just that little bit different → p. 82

⭐ **Tabasco**
Where boys will be boys → p. 83

⭐ **Central Park**
Open-air disco → p. 83

⭐ **Meccanò**
Popular haunt of Florentine disco fans → p. 84

⭐ **Tenax**
Top international DJs set Tenax buzzing with music from minimal via techno to house → p. 84

⭐ **Yab**
Disco must in the centre is also a good place for dinner → p. 84

⭐ **Teatro del Maggio Musicale Fiorentino**
Main stage for concerts, opera and ballet during the Maggio Musicale, the biggest cultural event in the city calendar → p. 85

⭐ **Teatro della Pergola**
Top-flight ensembles make for unforgettable evenings of music and drama in a historic setting → p. 85

MARCO POLO HIGHLIGHTS

DORIS (123 E4) *(⚏ G5)*

Trendy club with a hang towards house music. Most of the clientele are locals. *Daily from 10pm | Via Pandolfini 26r| www.dorisfirenze.it*

MARACANÀ (122 B2) *(⚏ F4)*

Brazil sets the tone here: from South American food, through the ambient rhythms to the usual evening show. *Mid-Sept–May Wed, Fri/Sat 8.30pm–4am | Via Faenza 4 | Tel. 0 55 21 02 98*

LOW BUDGET

▶ In many bars during happy hour from around 7pm you can enjoy an *aperitivo* and get a bite to eat from the buffet – almost for free: small snacks, pasta, rice dishes, salads and lots more besides. The 'banquets' are particularly sumptuous at *Kitsch 2* **(126 A5)** *(⚏ G3)* *(daily 6pm–3am | Via San Gallo 20r)*, at *Plaz* **(123 F4)** *(⚏ H5)* on the pretty Piazza de' Ciompi, a safe bet from breakfast right through to nightcap time *(daily aperitif from 6.30pm–10pm | Via Pietrapiana 26r)* and directly on the Arno at trendy *Noir* **(122 B4)** *(⚏ F5)* *(daily noon–3am | Lungarno Corsini 12r | www.noirfirenze.com)*.

▶ Unfortunately by no means the norm in Florentine discos: You can get in the popular *Twice Club* **(123 E5)** *(⚏ G5)* for free. Atmosphere and music are unbeatable! *Daily from 7pm | Via Verdi 57r | www.twiceclub.com*

▶ Wednesday is film day; admission is only 5 euros.

MECCANÒ ⭐ (124 B6) *(⚏ C4)*

All summer long, this is the all-time favourite disco-cum-pub-cum-restaurant in the *Parco delle Cascine*. *May–Sept Thu–Sat | Viale degli Olmi 1 | Tel. 0 55 33 13 71 | www.meccanofirenze.com*

PLASMA (130 C4) *(⚏ H6)*

Even if dancing is not your strong point, it's worth coming here: Until 10pm you get an *aperitivo* for 8 euros, consisting of a first-rate cocktail and a delicious small snack. After that, you could still decide to head on down the stairs to the dance floor ... *Wed–Sun 7pm–2am | Piazza Ferrucci 1*

TENAX ⭐ (133 D2)

This disco is a household name all over Italy. International DJs and a different programme every day. *Oct–May Thu–Sat from 10pm | Via Pratese 46 | www.tenax.org*

UNIVERSALE (U A4) *(⚏ D5)*

Club with good cocktail menu in a former cinema. Admission: 10–18 euros, depending on the day and time. *Thu–Sun 8pm–3am | Via Pisana 77r*

YAB ⭐ (122 C4) *(⚏ F5)*

The absolute *über*-disco right in the centre of Florence. Aperitif, evening meal and live music all rolled into one at 'You Are Beautiful'. *Wed–Sat and Mon from 9.30pm | Via dei Sassetti 5r | Tel. 0 55 21 51 60 | www.yab.it*

CONCERTS

AUDITORIUM FLOG (133 E3)

Lots of live concerts, mostly pop and rock, but also reggae, hip-hop and blues. Thu, Fri and Sat parties with good DJs. At 5–20 euros, admission prices are reasonable. Open-air cinema in summer. *Oct–May | Via M. Mercati 24b | Tel. 0 55 47 79 78 | www.flog.it*

PALASPORT (127 E5) *(ⓜ K4)*

Biggest location in the city, staging not only sporting events, but also shows by national and international music stars. *Viale Pasquale Paoli 3 | Tel. 0 55 67 88 41 | www.mandelaforum.it*

TEATRO DELLA PERGOLA ★ (123 E3) *(ⓜ G4)*

Historical theatre dating back to 1755, in which chamber concerts and plays are staged. *Via della Pergola 18 | Tel. 05 52 26 43 53 | www.teatrodellapergola.com*

Ballet, theatre, opera, pop & jazz – something for everyone at the historic Teatro Verdi

SASCHALL (U E5) *(ⓜ M6)*

On the site of the original 1970s Teatro Tenda, today's building still resembles a giant tent and still offers an up-to-the-minute concert and show programme. *Lungarno Aldo Moro 3 | Tel. 05 56 50 41 12 | www.saschall.it*

TEATRO DEL MAGGIO MUSICALE FIORENTINO ★ (124 C6) *(ⓜ D4)*

Large opera and concert hall for performances during the *Maggio Musicale* event. Work is due to be completed in 2012 on a new building in the *Parco della Musica e della Cultura* (124 C5) *(ⓜ D4)*. *Corso Italia 16 | Tel. 05 52 77 93 50 | www.maggiofiorentino.com*

TEATRO VERDI (123 E4) *(ⓜ G5)*

Large theatre which forms the backdrop for concerts by the *Orchestra Regionale della Toscana. Via Ghibellina 99 | Tel. 0 55 21 23 20 | www.teatroverdifirenze.it, www.orchestradellatoscana.it*

THEATRE

Florentines spend more money on visits to the theatre than any of their compatriots. Alongside traditional theatres, many small companies have established themselves in the city, from chamber theatre and experimental drama to various performances – in summer, also in the gardens and courtyards of palaces and monasteries. Performances during the *Estate Fiesolana (see 'Festivals & Events', p. 105))*, which usually take place in the *Teatro Romano*, the grand Roman theatre in Fiesole, are highly impressive. You can find details of programmes in the daily newspapers La Nazione *(www.lanazione. it)* and La Repubblica *(www.repubblica.it)*.

EX-STAZIONE LEOPOLDA
(124 C5) *(ꟼ D3–4)*
Since the 1990s, the huge halls of the former station have been the location for exhibitions, diverse happenings and performances and also the international theatre festival which takes place in May. *Viale Fratelli Rosselli 5 | www.stazione-leopolda.com*

INSIDER TIP ODEON CINEHALL
(122 B4) *(ꟼ F5)*
A delight for cinemagoers – even those who do not understand Italian – as every Mon, Tue and Wed, films are screened here in the original language. Not only can you enjoy the film, but the surroundings are a treat, too: a beautiful film palace with a magical 1920s interior. An experience you'd be hard put to repeat anywhere else these days. *Piazza Strozzi 2 | Tel. 0 55 29 50 51 | www.cinehall.it*

INSIDER TIP TEATRO DEL SALE
(130 B2) *(ꟼ H5)*
A theatre and, at the same time, a restaurant and delicatessen: Once you've purchased your membership card for 5

BOOKS & FILMS

▶ **Brunelleschi's Dome: The Story of the Great Cathedral in Florence** – Architecture and intrigue: Ross King tells how the finest dome in the world was built.

▶ **The Marshal's Own Case and The Marshall and the Madwoman** – Both detective novels by Magdalena Nabb capture the local atmosphere and give you a glimpse of the darker side of the city.

▶ **Macchiavelli: A Biography** – Lively account by Miles J. Unger of the Florentine diplomat, civil servant and most infamous political strategist of his time.

▶ **A Room with a View** – James Ivory's film account of a love story at the turn of the century was rewarded with three Oscars – and filmed at several locations in Florence, such as the Piazza della Signoria and the Fattoria di Maiano.

▶ **Tea with Mussolini** – Franco Zeffirelli made this autobiographical film about the fate of English 'Florentines' at the end of the war. Backdrop was the city centre, the surrounding hills and San Gimignano.

▶ **Portrait of a Lady** – Nicole Kidman and John Malkovich are the main protagonists in the filming of Henry James' novel of the same name by Jane Campion.

▶ **Fireworks (Fuochi d'artificio)** – Typical Florentine mentality and language in the film by Leonardo Pieraccioni (with English subtitles).

▶ **Hannibal** – The fact that Hannibal Lecter turns up again in Florence of all places was a not insignificant factor in the success of Ridley Scott's thriller.

The Teatro del Sale is a marriage of culinary and dramatic art

euros at the door, you can brunch, lunch or dine in these evocative surroundings, seated in leather armchairs, surrounded by old bookcases or in full view of the kitchen. In the evening, you can even experience the king of Florentine cuisine, Fabio Picchi, as he himself serves you your food (it is wise to be there from around 7pm!). Sometimes you share a large table with complete strangers; at others, it's so cramped on the tiny benches that you can't even put your glass down.

Shortly before 9pm, the tables are pushed together, and the performance begins. You can get more information about the current programme before you go from the Internet. Even without a show, an evening here is sure to be an unforgettable experience. *Tue–Sat 9am–11am, 12.30pm–2.30pm and 7.30pm–9pm; show from 9pm; closed Aug | Brunch: 7 euros; lunch: 20 euros;* *dinner: 30 euros | Via dei Macci 111r | Tel. 05 52 00 14 92 | www.teatrodelsale.com*

TEATRO DELLA LIMONAIA (133 E2)
They've been playing avant-garde theatre in the suburb of Sesto Fiorentino since 1987. Performances take place in the elegant orangery of the Villa Corsi Salviati. *Via Gramsci 426 | Tel. 0 55 44 08 52 | www. teatrodellalimonaia.it*

TEATRO PUCCINI (133 D3) *(M B2)*
Highly popular with local residents, this venue offers a colourful programme, ranging from satirical cabaret to musicals. *Piazza Puccini/Via delle Cascine 41 | Tel. 0 55 36 20 67 | www.teatropuccini.it*

TEATRO DI RIFREDI (133 E3)
Musicals and experimental theatre, performed in the suburb of Rifredi. *Via V. Emanuele II 303 | Tel. 05 54 22 03 61 | www.toscanateatro.it*

WHERE TO STAY

The key to any Florence trip is to book early! Be sure to take the season into account, too: In high summer, it is advisable to escape to a hotel out in the countryside, rather than remain in town if you want to stay a little longer.

If you are staying in the centre, however, you can return to your hotel for a while around midday when Florence is at its hottest and experience the city and its residents at first hand.

Are you bringing your family with you to Florence? If so, you'll find plenty of information at *Italy Family Hotels (Tel. 05 41 39 48 51 | www.italyfamilyhotels. com). Waytostay,* on the other hand, offers holiday apartments *(www.waytostay. com/Florence).* Details of good, value-for-money accommodation is to be had from *Florence Promhotels (Tel. 0 55 55 39 41 |*

www.promhotels.it). The *Consorzio Informazioni Turistiche Alberghiere (www. firenzealbergo.it)* carries out free hotel reservations. The brochure entitled *Guida all'ospitalità,* containing information on all accommodation in Florence and the surrounding area, is available free of charge from the tourist information office *(www.firenzeturismo.it).*

HOTELS: EXPENSIVE

BRUNELLESCHI (123 D4) *(㋡ F5)*
Spend the night in one of the oldest buildings in the city, with its tower from the Byzantine era. Modern and luxuriously furnished, with a good restaurant and located in the heart of the city. *96 rooms | Piazza S. Elisabetta 3 | Tel. 05 52 73 70 | www.hotelbrunelleschi.it*

Photo: Palazzo Galletti

Would you prefer to bed down in a historical city palace, designer hotel, a B & B or a family-sized villa out in the sticks?

EXECUTIVE (125 D6) (*𝄞 D4*)
Elegant hotel on the Arno. Some rooms even have their own private sauna. Car parking at extra cost. *48 rooms | Via Curtatone 5 | Tel. 0 55 21 74 51 | www.hotel executive.it*

GALLERY HOTEL ART ⭐ (122 C5) (*𝄞 F5*)
Designer hotel near the Ponte Vecchio. In the lobby, bar and library, occasional exhibitions of modern art. On the shady piazzetta, treat yourself to a few delicious nibbles from the *Fusion Bar (Shozan Gallery)*. Japanese/international cuisine *(closed Aug)*. *74 rooms* INSIDER TIP *(nos. 701, 707 and 708 with roof terrace!) | Vicolo dell'Oro 3–5 | Tel. 0 55 27 26 40 00 | www.galleryhotelart.com*

GRAND HOTEL MINERVA
(122 A2–3) (*𝄞 E4*)
Central location, quiet rooms at the rear. Warm, welcoming service and a beautiful swimming pool on the roof. Incidentally, even if you're not staying at the hotel, you can enjoy an aperitif at the substantial buffet by the pool on Thursdays INSIDER TIP at *Minerva Giò*,

including live music, for just 15 euros *(mid–May–beg. Aug 7.30pm–10pm)*! *102 rooms | Piazza S. Maria Novella 16 | Tel. 05 52 72 30 | www.grandhotelminerva. com*

INSIDER TIP ▶ **PALAZZO GUADAGNI** (122 A6) *(M E6)*
Sleep in this 16th-century Renaissance palace and fall under the spell of the sensational view from the roof garden. Delight-

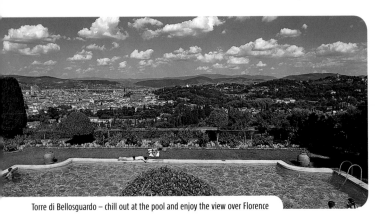

Torre di Bellosguardo – chill out at the pool and enjoy the view over Florence

HH FLORENCE (130 B3) *(M H6)*
Pure, unadulterated luxury, not just for honeymooners. At this 'Hotel Home', everything – tables, chairs, floors, beds – is dazzling white, with a touch of gold here and there. Large panorama terrace. *39 rooms | Piazza Piave 3 | Tel. 0 55 24 36 68 | www.hhflorence.it*

JK PLACE (122 A3) *(M E4)*
A very elegant, intimate hotel, oozing with charm and style on the spacious Piazza S. Maria Novella. *20 rooms | Piazza S. Maria Novella 7 | Tel. 05 52 64 51 81 | www. jkplace.com*

LUNGARNO ★ ⋇ (122 B5) *(M F5)*
Modern and luxurious, located on the south bank of the Arno. Excellent restaurant *(closed Aug)*. *73 rooms | Borgo S. Jacopo 14 | Tel. 0 55 27 26 40 00 | www. lungarnohotels.com*

ful rooms with typical Florentine flair. *15 rooms | Piazza Santo Spirito 9 | Tel. 05 52 65 83 76 | www.palazzoguadagni.com*

TORNABUONI 1 (122 B4) *(M F5)*
Exquisite hotel with fabulous views from the large terrace. *22 rooms | Via Tornabuoni 1 | Tel. 05 52 65 81 61 | www.tornabuoni1.com*

TORRE DI BELLOSGUARDO ★ ⋇ (128 B4) *(M C6)*
Tranquillity and hospitality in a fine Renaissance villa, overlooking the city from the south. Spacious park with pool. *16 rooms | Via Roti Michelozzi 2 | Tel. 05 52 29 81 45 | www.torrebellosguardo.com*

VILLA CARLOTTA ★ (129 D5) *(M E7)*
Elegant yet welcoming atmosphere in a 19th-century villa on the green slopes above the Porta Romana. *33 rooms | Via Michele di Lando 3 | Tel. 0 55 22 05 30 | www.hotelvillacarlotta.it*

HOTELS: MODERATE

ANNALENA ⭐ (129 D4) (🛱 E6)
Romantic boutique hotel in a prime location near the Boboli Gardens. The prettiest rooms lead off the open gallery and have views onto the hotel garden. *20 rooms | Via Romana 34 | Tel. 0 55 22 24 02 | www.annalenahotel.com*

APE ROSA ⭐ (125 E1) (🛱 F1)
This 19th-century villa has six lovingly furnished rooms, and its delightful, quiet location makes this B & B an ideal place to escape the chaos of downtown Florence. Own car park and Italian-style garden. *Via dei Cappuccini 12 | Tel. 0 55 47 51 78 | www.aperosa.it*

APRILE (125 D6) (🛱 E4)
Enchanting hotel in the Palazzo del Borgo, with tasteful furnishings and wonderful garden. *34 rooms | Via della Scala 6 | Tel. 0 55 21 62 37 | www.hotelaprile.it*

ARTI & HOTEL (123 E2) (🛱 G4)
Small boutique hotel, with prettily furnished rooms, close to the Piazza SS. Annunziata. *11 rooms | Via dei Servi 38a | Tel. 05 52 67 85 53 | www.artiehotel.it*

BENCISTÀ ⭐ ⚜ (U E2) (🛱 N2)
This stylish family hotel is located halfway to Fiesole, on a hillside amidst olive groves. Friendly atmosphere and a fabulous view over the city. 6 km (4 miles) from the city centre. *40 rooms | Mar–Nov | Fiesole | Via Benedetto da Maiano 4 | Tel. 05 55 91 63 | www.bencista.com*

CELLAI (125 F5) (🛱 F3)
Tasteful rooms, furnished with antiques and much attention to detail. Pretty roof terrace and cosy lounge with an open fireplace. *55 rooms | Via XVII Aprile 14 | Tel. 0 55 48 92 91 | www.hotelcellai.it*

LOGGIATO DEI SERVITI ⭐ (123 E1) (🛱 G4)
Charming hotel, loaded with character, in a former guesthouse of the Servite Order.

⭐ **Gallery Hotel Art**
Fine hotel in great location; sometimes transformed into a gallery → p. 89

⭐ **Lungarno**
Modern and tasteful, right by the Ponte Vecchio → p. 90

⭐ **Torre di Bellosguardo**
Renaissance villa with pool, park and panoramic view over the city → p. 90

⭐ **Villa Carlotta**
Charming country-house flair, close to the centre → p. 90

⭐ **Annalena**
Bijou domicile near the Boboli Gardens → p. 91

⭐ **Ape Rosa**
Pleasant atmosphere in a quietly situated villa → p. 91

⭐ **Bencistà**
Villa with an informal touch in the hills of Fiesole → p. 91

⭐ **Loggiato dei Serviti**
Bags of character in the rooms of a former monastery → p. 91

⭐ **Morandi alla Crocetta**
Stylish, charming and, believe it or not, affordable → p. 92

⭐ **Fattoria di Maiano**
Holiday between art and olives, on the actual set of A Room with a View → p. 94

MARCO POLO HIGHLIGHTS

HOTELS: MODERATE

It is situated on one of the most beautiful squares in Florence. *38 rooms | Piazza della SS. Annunziata 3 | Tel. 0 55 28 95 92 | www.loggiatodeiservitihotel.it*

MORANDI ALLA CROCETTA ★
(123 F1) (*📖 G4*)
Small, stylish, relatively quiet hotel in a former monastery, close to SS. Anunziata. Ideal for families. Garage at extra cost. *10 rooms | Via Laura 50 | Tel. 05 52 34 47 47 | www.hotelmorandi.it*

ORTO DEI MEDICI (125 F5) (*📖 G3*)
Pleasant hotel in the centre, with pretty rooms, delightful garden and a car park. *42 rooms | Via San Gallo 30 | Tel. 0 55 48 34 27 | www.ortodeimedici.it*

PALAZZO GALLETTI (123 E3) (*📖 G5*)
This pleasant B & B, with every creature comfort, is located on the first floor of a 19th-century palace. *11 rooms | Via S. Egidio 12 | Tel. 05 53 90 57 50 | www.palazzogalletti.it*

RIVA LOFTS (124 A6) (*📖 B4*)
Eight modern studios between 30 and 100 m^2 (36 and 120 yd^2) in size, with a garden and pool, right on the south bank of the Arno. *Via Baccio Bandinelli 98 | Tel. 05 57 13 02 72 | www.rivalofts.com*

LUXURY HOTELS

Excelsior (129 D2) (*📖 E5*)
Traditional hotel in an elegant 19th-century building on the banks of the Arno. 🍃 Beautiful panorama terrace. From 620 euros. *171 rooms and suites | Piazza Ognissanti 3 | Tel. 05 52 71 51 | www.starwoodhotels.com*

FOUR SEASONS HOTEL
(126 B5) (*📖 G–H 3–4*)
Only the best is good enough: the location, the palace, with its 4.5 ha (11 acres) park, the restaurant Il Palagio and the ● excellent spa! *117 rooms | Borgo Pinti 99 | Tel. 05 52 62 61 | www.fourseasons.com/florence*

Helvetia & Bristol (122 B3) (*📖 F5*)
Stylish town hotel, oozing with old English charm. Beautiful, antique furniture and an enchanting conservatory. From 330 euros. *67 rooms and apartments | Via dei Pescioni 2 | Tel. 05 52 66 51 | www.royaldemeure.com*

Savoy (122 C3) (*📖 F5*)
Ideal for luxury shoppers: Grand Hotel, taken over by Sir Rocco Forte and located right in the city centre, with a view over the Piazza della Repubblica. Superb service and a fine restaurant. From 330 euros. *102 rooms and suites | Piazza della Repubblica 7 | Tel. 05 52 73 51 | www.hotelsavoy.it*

Villa San Michele 🍃 (U E2)
This monastery on the slopes below Fiesole was designed in part by Michelangelo and rates as one of the most luxurious in Italy. Magnificent view of the city, both from the hotel itself and from the pool. The villa is surrounded by a spacious park. In the loggia, you can enjoy an excellent meal, or simply drink a cocktail! 780–2500 euros. *46 rooms and apartments | Closed mid-Nov–mid-Mar | Fiesole | Via Doccia 4 | Tel. 05 55 67 82 00 | www.villasanmichele.com*

Luxury awaits you behind Michelangelo's façade: Villa San Michele near Fiesole

INSIDER TIP ▶ ROYAL (125 F4) *(𝄞 F3)*
Situated in a 19th-century villa, with a large garden and pool. Quiet and yet not far from the station. *39 rooms | Via delle Ruote 50–54 | Tel. 0 55 48 32 87 | www. hotelroyalfirenze.it*

HOTELS: BUDGET

ALESSANDRA ♨ (122 B5) *(𝄞 F5)*
Hotel with large rooms; numbers 21, 22 and 26 also have a view of the Arno. *27 rooms | Closed 2 weeks mid-Dec and mid-Aug | Borgo SS. Apostoli 17 | Tel. 0 55 28 34 38 | www.hotelalessandra.com*

BOBOLI (129 D4) *(𝄞 E6)*
Close to the Boboli Gardens; modest, cosy and good value for money. *21 rooms | Via Romana 63 | Tel. 0 55 23 36 51 8 | www. hotelboboli.com*

CLASSIC (129 E5) *(𝄞 E7)*
Hotel in a typical 19th-century Florentine villa, with garden. Close to Porta Romana. Car park. *20 rooms | Closed Aug | Viale Machiavelli 25 | Tel. 0 55 22 93 51 | www.classichotel.it*

GIOIA (125 F5) *(𝄞 G3)*
Small hotel right in the heart of town, with tastefully furnished rooms. Garage at extra cost. *28 rooms | Via Cavour 25 | Tel. 0 55 28 28 04 | www.hotelgioia.it*

HOTEL ARIZONA (130 B2) *(𝄞 H5)*
Just a stone's throw from the bustling Sant'Ambrogio market, and yet very quiet. Garage at extra cost. *21 rooms | Via Farini 2 | Tel. 0 55 24 53 21 | www. arizonahotel.it*

HOTEL LA SCALETTA (122 B6) *(𝄞 F6)*
The rooms are pleasantly cool in summer, and there's a roof terrace for romantic dinners! Friendly service. *15 rooms | Via Guicciardini 13 | Tel. 0 55 28 30 28 | www. lascaletta.com*

How fitting: James Ivory filmed A Room with a View at the Fattoria di Maiano

HOTEL VILLA BONELLI (U E1)
Charming stopover in the hills of Fiesole. *22 rooms | April–Nov | Fiesole | Via Poeti 3 | Tel. 05 55 95 13 | www.hotelvilla bonelli.com*

POR S. MARIA (122 C4) (∭ F5)
Cosy rooms with a view over the hustle and bustle of the city. *8 rooms (only one with bathroom) | Via Calimaruzza 3 | Tel. 0 55 216370 | www.hotelporsantamaria. com*

AGRITOURISM/B & B

Tips for bed & breakfast and agritourism are to be had from *AB&BA (www.abba-firenze.it)* and *www.agriturismo.regione. toscana.it*

INSIDER TIP A TEATRO (123 E4) (∭ G5)
Enchanting B & B giving top value for money, right next to the Teatro Verdi. *6 rooms | Via Verdi 12 | 4th floor, lift available | Tel. 05 52 63 82 42 | www.a-teatro.com*

B & B ALBERGHINO ☆ (125 D5) (∭ E3)
Antiques lover Letizia takes care of her guests as if they were friends: She gives restaurant tips, helps with ticket reservations and always knows what's going on where. *5 rooms | Via Cittadella 6a | Tel. 05 53 31 42 | www.alberghino.it*

B & B CAPRI MOON (122 A4) (∭ E5)
Pleasant atmosphere, located on one of Florence's exclusive shopping streets. *4 rooms | Via della Vigna Nuova 17 | Tel. 05 52 39 64 15 | www.caprimoon.com*

FATTORIA DI MAIANO ★ ☆ (U F2)
Twelve cosy apartments in the grounds of a 15th-century monastery which has often been used as a film set. Swimming pool. Restaurant which uses ingredients from its own production and a small farm. Bookable only by the week; for two persons, approx. 800 euros. *Fiesole | Via Benedetto da Maiano 11 | Tel. 0 55 59 96 00 | www. fattoriadimaiano.com*

MARY'S HOUSE (125 D6) (*E4*)
This family-run stopover offers modest accommodation; some rooms share a bathroom. Located on the second floor of the building, though no lift available. *6 rooms | Via della Scala 43 | www.marys house.it*

PALAZZO RUSPOLI (133 E2)
Charming, very pleasant B & B, with rooms of varying sizes, directly on the cathedral square. Friendly staff and a good breakfast. *20 rooms | Via Martelli 5 | Tel. 05 52 67 05 63 | www.palazzo-ruspoli.it*

INSIDER TIP **RELAIS IL CESTELLO** (129 D2) (*E5*)
On the south bank of the Arno, pretty B & B on a piazzetta, looking out onto the river. *10 rooms | Piazza di Cestello 9 | Tel. 0 55 28 06 32 | www.relaisilcestello.it*

RESIDENZA IL CARMINE (129 D3) (*E6*)
Six prettily furnished apartments (four give onto the garden courtyard, with sitting area) with bathroom and cooking facilities for 2–4 persons. Ideal also for a longer stay. Quiet, but located in the lively district of Santo Spirito. Minimum stay, three nights. *Via d'Ardiglione 28 | Tel. 05 52 38 20 60 | www.residenzailcarmine. com*

LE TRE STANZE (123 E3) (*G5*)
Right round the corner from the cathedral, this quirky B & B has a garden and a warm welcome from host, Beny Steiner. *3 rooms | Via dell'Oriuolo 43 | Tel. 05 52 12 87 56 | www.letrestanze.it*

CAMPING

CAMPING PANORAMICO FIESOLE
(133 E2)
Small quiet campsite, with a view over Florence and a beautiful pool. *Mid-Mar–Oct | Fiesole | Via Peramonda 1 | Tel. 0 55 59 90 69 | www.florencecamping. com*

CAMPING VILLAGE MICHELANGELO (130 B4) (*H6–7*)
Campsite in an idyllic location directly below the Piazzale Michelangelo, where you can also hire tents between April and September. You can reach the site by bus (no. 12). *Viale Michelangelo 80 | Tel. 05 56 81 19 77 | www.camping.it/ toscana/michelangelo*

LOW BUDGET

▶ The three youth hostels worth recommending are the *Ostello Villa Camerata* **(127 F3)** (*L1*), out in the countryside, but just 10 minutes away from the cathedral by bus (no. 11) *(rooms for two, three or more persons: 18–30 euros/ pers. incl. breakfast | Viale Augusto Righi 2–4 | Tel. 0 55 60 14 51 | www. ostellofirenze.it)*; the *Ostello Santa Monica* **(129 D3)** (*E5*) in a former monastery close to Santa Maria del Carmine in the district of Oltrarno *(dormitories: 18–25 euros/pers. | Via Santa Monica 6 | Tel. 0 55 26 83 38 | www.ostello.it)* and the *Plus Florence* **(125 F4)** (*F3*) *(double rooms and dormitories: 20–30 euros/pers. | Via S. Caterina D'Alessandria 15 | Tel. 05 54 62 89 34 | www.plusflorence. com)*.

▶ Bed & Breakfast is an alternative to the steadily rising hotel prices in Florence. Reservations via *www. bbplanet.it* and *www.bed-and-break fast-italien.com*.

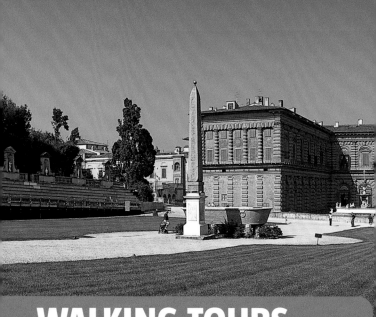

WALKING TOURS

The tours are marked in green in the street atlas,
the pull-out map and on the back cover

1 **FROM SANTA MARIA
NOVELLA OVER THE
SOUTHERN HILLSIDES**

Sit back and relax and see
the city from the seat of a
bus. With the biglietto 24 ore
for 5 euros (available from
tobacconist's and kiosks and to be validated on the bus) you can travel back-
wards and forwards across town for 24
hours. The journey time itself is around
60 minutes, but plan at least half a day
for stops.

Bus route no. 12 starts at the Piazza della
Stazione close to the main entrance to
the railway station **S. Maria Novella**
→ p. 49. If you start your tour of the
green and romantic side of Florence
before 9am, you are sure to get a seat

by the window! The buses run every 20
minutes. As you cross the river, you have
a magnificent view down the Arno. After a few bends, the city wall comes into
view, which encloses the old craftsmen's
district of San Frediano.

Leave the bus at the 'Pratolini' stop, the
tenth after the bridge; you are now
standing on the Piazza Tasso. From here,
you can walk along the old ☾ city wall
towards the imposing **Porta Romana**. If
you have planned ahead, you can now
visit the largest private garden within
the Florentine city walls, the English-
style **Giardino Torrigiani** *(by prior ap-
pointment, for groups of over 15 people |
20 euros/pers. | Via dei Serragli 144 | Tel.
0 55 22 45 27)*. If you wish to leave out
this detour, continue with the bus to the

Photo: Palazzo Pitti with the Giardino di Boboli

On foot, by bus, onto the slopes to the north or south – Florence is just waiting to be explored

city gate, the Porta Romana, which was built in 1326.

If you like walking, you should take a stroll from here uphill along the tree-lined ☀ Viale Niccolò Machiavelli. After about 25 minutes, taking in views of villas, gardens and finally the whole city, you reach the Piazzale Galileo. The bus takes three minutes for the same route and stops here.

Now you have three possibilities: You can either carry on walking for 100 m (110yd), then turn left and embark on the half-

hour trek along the Via di S. Leonardo, between villas and gardens and past the ☀ Forte di Belvedere → p. 53.

After a few metres you can visit the ● enchanting, 40,000-m² (48,000-yd²) garden of the Villa Bardini on the right, which has finally, after 40 years, been restored and opened to the public. Enjoy the great views from the ☀ Rondò Belvedere and take in the wisteria-clad tunnel and the many species of hydrangea. The finest panoramic view of all, however, is to be had from the long

Baroque staircase *(opening times and admission prices, see Giardino di Boboli | Costa San Giorgio 2, entrance also in Via dei Bardi 1r | www.bardinipeyron.it)*. Either you take the lower exit of the garden and turn left along the **Via dei Bardi** towards the Ponte Vecchio or, higher up, follow the steep **Costa San Giorgio** down to the Piazza S. Maria Sopr'Arno.

A second alternative is to walk straight on from the **Restaurant Châlet Fontana** for approximately 1 km (1 2/3 mi) along the ☼ scenic Viale Galileo Galilei, with a view onto the **Forte di Belvedere**, down to the Arno as it winds through the city and over to the hillsides around San Domenico and Fiesole, rising up in the distance. On the right-hand side, on slightly higher ground, you can see the marble façade of **San Miniato al Monte** → p. 59. Take this opportunity to admire this beautiful church, before you continue on the final metres down to the ☼ **Piazzale Michelangelo** → p. 58.

The third variation also begins at the **Châlet Fontana**, where you get on the no. 12 bus again and enjoy the view on the journey down. The buses stop for around five to ten minutes on the Piazzale Michelangelo (final stop!) – time enough for a photo of the INSIDER TIP panorama before you.

If you arrived here on the bus, this is where you really should get out and walk down to the **Porta San Niccolò** along the pretty **Viale Poggi**. If you happen to be visiting the city in May, you are in luck and should make a point of seeing the **Giardino dell'Iris** – an absolute must,

The finest view over the city is to be had from the Piazzale Michelangelo

as it is only open in this month. It is the location for the annual International Iris Competition, in honour of the 'Florentine lily', the heraldic flower of Florence. At this time, some 1500 iris are in full bloom (*www.irisfirenze.it*).

If you have already covered a substantial part of the way to Piazzale Michelangelo on foot, you can relax on the bus and ride down the beautiful Viale Michelangelo. Get out at the fifth stop (Ferrucci 04) on the piazza of the same name and stretch your legs a little by strolling along the bank of the Arno towards the Ponte Vecchio. After the next bridge, the Ponte alle Grazie, you pass the small Chiesa Evangelica Luterana, built at the end of the 19th century for the Lutheran community in the city. Piazza S. Maria Sopr'Arno, directly on the river, is the Golden View Open Bar (*Via dei Bardi 58 | Tel. 0 55 21 45 02 | www.goldenview openbar.com*), whose name does not disappoint and which makes an excellent place to round off your day. If you're feeling a little tired, just hop on the electric minibus D at the Piazza Ferrucci which will take you back to the Ponte Vecchio.

2 BY BUS TO SAN DOMENICO AND FIESOLE

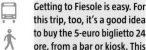

Getting to Fiesole is easy. For this trip, too, it's a good idea to buy the 5-euro biglietto 24 ore, from a bar or kiosk. This lets you get on and off the bus as you wish along the way. Bus no. 7 departs from the Piazza San Marco/Via La Pira. If you get on here, you're almost certain to get a seat. The journey time to Fiesole is around 30 minutes. Plan 1–3 hours to do some sightseeing.

After a short ride through the prosperous suburbs, the road begins to climb, skirted by villas, gardens and olive groves. Half-

way up, you come to the village of San Domenico, a group of houses clustered around the Monastery Church of San Domenico which dates back to the beginning of the 15th century (altered in the 17th century). Leave the bus here. Opposite the church, the narrow, steep Via di Badia leads down into the Mugnone valley. After a few metres, the Badia Fiesolana appears on the left; an impressive Romanesque structure which was the cathedral church of Fiesole until 1026. Today, it houses the European University Institute (*www.iue.it*), a post-doctoral research facility.

The ⛰ scenic road continues upwards, offering views across the city as far as the hills of the Chianti region in the south and to the ridge of the Pratomagno in the east, sometimes still covered in snow in springtime. After the tight hairpin bend, the loggia of the hotel ⛰ Villa San Michele → p. 66 comes into view on the slope to the right. Michelangelo had a hand in the designs for this former monastery. The location is priceless; the hotel, too, unfortunately. After the final bend, the bus comes to a halt on the piazza in ★ Fiesole.

On the square, the overwhelming Duomo San Romolo (built to commemorate St Romulus in 1028–56) and the stately Seminary to the northwest are impossible to overlook. The Palazzo Vescovile (Archbishop's Palace), with its fine staircase and so untypically Tuscan palm trees, seems almost to have been pushed into the corner. Between the seminary and the palace, a road leads up to the monastery of ● ⛰ San Francesco, dated 1330. Back in the days of Etruscan rule, an acropolis stood on this spot, INSIDER TIP at 345 m (378yd), the highest in the area. The whole of Florence lies literally at your feet.

Back on the Piazza Mino da Fiesole, you

can recover from the climb in one of the many restaurants. A good choice is the **Perseus** *(daily | Piazza Mino da Fiesole 9 | Tel. 05 55 91 43 | Moderate)*, with its pretty inner courtyard. Boutiques, shops selling fine ceramics, foods and shoes are strung out along the length of the lous **Teatro Romano**, which once seated 3000 people, is still a favoured venue for summer INSIDER TIP theatre and ballet performances during the *Estate Fiesolana → p. 105*. Don't miss the exhibition of archaeological finds made here, now in the adjacent museum.

Fiesole: Roman theatre, with the Mugnone valley as the backdrop

Piazza. A rare sight is the tiny **barber's shop run by Lino**: Gentlemen can treat themselves to an old-fashioned wet shave for just 8 euros! At the highest point on the square is the **Town Hall**, decorated with numerous heraldic crests, and next to it the small church of **Santa Maria Primerana**, which dates back to the 16th century. In front are equestrian statues of the king, Vittorio Emanuele II, and Garibaldi, father of the united Italy. Passing the apse of the cathedral, you come to the prettily situated **Area Archeologica**. Significant finds from Etruscan and Roman times have been unearthed on this 30,000-m^2 (36,000- yd^2) site, including the remains of temples and thermal baths. The fabu-

Opposite the entrance, directly behind the cathedral, is the **Museo Bandini,** with its small, but impressive collection of works by Florentine artists of the 13th–15th centuries. *(Area and Museo Archeologico, Teatro Romano and Museo Bandini: Mar, Oct daily 10am–6pm, April–Sept daily 10am–7pm, Nov–Feb Wed–Mon 10am–2pm | Joint ticket: 10 euros | www.fiesolemusei.it)*. Lovers of modern art should head off to the Via Giovanni Dupré, 100m (110yd) further downhill, where the **Museo Fondazione Primo Conti** (signposted) is situated. This delightful little villa contains a comprehensive collection, including works by Italian Futurists *(Mon–Fri 9am–1pm | Admission: 3 euros | www.fondazioneprimoconti.org)*.

3

FROM DESIGNER FASHIONS TO DOLCI – SHOP LIKE A FLORENTINE

When in Florence, do as the Florentines do – or, rather, shop like one. Make your way eastwards out of the city centre, starting at the Piazza della Repubblica.

Stroll out of town along the bustling Via del Corso, past the small 16th-century church of Santa Maria de' Ricci; the frequent sound of classical music from inside makes you want to stop for a moment to listen. Little boutiques and enoteche entice you in to buy. The range of upmarket fashion labels at Matucci is very tempting; Fabriano sells the finest writing instruments; at the Galleria del Chianti you'll find not only good wines, but also olive oil and other delicious foods.

Continue your stroll straight ahead along the shady Borgo degli Albizi, past the lavish Palazzo Ramirez Montalvo, now the home of the famous auctioneer's Pandolfini. Opposite, you can choose yourself a wedding dress at Atelier Aimée, and if you like your everyday clothes extravagant, pop in to Ethic, a few steps further on. Are you a ceramics fan? If so, make a detour through the tiny Arco di San Pierino, before your reach the Piazza Salvemini, to Sbigoli Terrecotte → p. 74. On the piazza itself is Vestrini, a paradise for chocolate junkies!

Following the Via Pietrapiana, you gradually leave the centre. The flea market on the Piazza dei Ciompi to your right is an invitation to rummage for some bargains. Time for lunch? A little further on, you can still your hunger at Rocco's stand in the old market hall, the Mercato di Sant'Ambrogio → p. 77. The shopping street changes its name to Borgo la Croce, now lined with small shops and leading to the Piazza Beccaria, and the old city gate, the Porta della Croce. Before you dodge the traffic across the busy intersection, take a look at the tempting display in the window of the tiny confectioner's on the right-hand side, Dolci e Dolcezze.

The ● Via Gioberti, the Florentines' favourite shopping street, begins on the opposite side. Here, you'll find everything – honestly – from boutiques and jeweller's, book shops and the elegant shopping arcade, Le Nove Botteghe, baker's, butcher's, delicatessens, fishmonger's or supermarkets. In between there are several bars and trattoria and a number of very good enoteche, such as the Enoteca Bonatti. From the Piazza Beccaria you can take the electric minibus C2 back to the city centre.

Via del Corso

TRAVEL
WITH KIDS

In recent years, Florence has started paying more attention to children. The *Museo Zoologico 'La Specola'* → p. 54, for example, has a fascinating department dedicated to anatomical models and skeletons. Or perhaps you'd find the mummies at the *Museo Archeologico* more interesting → p. 42? If your kids are bursting with energy, you shouldn't miss the opportunity to climb up inside the bell tower or the cathedral dome → p. 30!

FRESH AIR FOR THE LITTLE ONES
Unfortunately, there are very few playgrounds in the city. Simple, but 'functional' could best describe the ones at the stadium (127 E4) (*ሠ K3*) *(Viale Manfredo Fanti)*, in the Giardino dell'Orticultura (126 A3) (*ሠ G2*) with its stunningly beautiful greenhouse *(daily 8.30am until sunset | Via Vittorio Emanuele 4)* and on the Piazza d'Azeglio (126 B6) (*ሠ H4*).

GET MOVING!
Milleunabici rent out bicycles (also with children's seats) at reasonable rates; on larger squares and at stations *(www. cooperativaulisse.org)*.
The open-air swimming pools are popular in summer, particularly with younger guests. They are the *Costoli* close to the stadium (127 E6) (*ሠ K4*) *(June–Aug Tue–Sun 10am–6pm, Mon 2pm–6pm | Admission: 7 euros, children under 6: free | Viale Paoli 9 | Tel. 05 56 23 60 27)* and the *Bellariva* (133 F3) (*ሠ L6*) *(June–Aug daily 10am–6pm | Admission: 7 euros, 7–13-year-olds: 5 euros | Lungarno Aldo Moro 6 | Tel. 0 55 67 75 21)*.

MUSEO DEI RAGAZZI
For children aged three and over, there are special guided tours and workshops in the Palazzo Vecchio, in S. Maria del Carmine and in the Cappella Brancacci, in the Museo Stibbert and the Museo Leonardiano di Vinci. The daily programme at the Palazzo Vecchio is extremely varied and also of interest to adults. It's worth coming for the terrific views from the building and the chance to take a look at the rooms and apartments you would not normally see! Don't miss the sensational *camminamento di ronda*, a walk along the 14th-century passageway used by the guards on patrol in the palace and, 42m (46yd) up, offering a great view of the Piazza della Signoria *(Mon–Sat 9.30am–5pm, Sun until 12.30pm | Book in advance, Tel. 05 52 76 82 24 | Admission: 6 euros, reduced: 2 euros | Informa-

What to do with the bambini – Tips on how to keep toddlers, mini sporting aces and juvenile explorers happy in Florence

tion at the Palazzo Vecchio | Piazza della Signoria 1 | www.museoragazzi.it).

INSIDER TIP **MUSEO STIBBERT**
(125 F1–2) (*ØJ F1*)

In 1860, Stibbert began putting together a veritable cabinet of curiosities. Sixty-four rooms in his house are full of furniture, sculptures, costumes and other unusual objects. The heart of the collection is made up of 10,000 suits of armour and weapons from Europe, Asia and Africa. The *Sala di Cavalcata,* which resembles a medieval knights' hall, features a parade of 14 knights and horses in full armour from the 16th century! The villa is surrounded by a spacious park, which is also a good place for a picnic. *Park: April–Oct Fri–Wed 8am–7pm, Nov–Mar Fri–Wed 8am–5pm | Free admission; Museum: all year round Mon–Wed 10am–2pm, Fri–Sun 10am–6pm | Admission: 6 euros, reduced: 4 euros | Via Stibbert 26 | www.museostibbert.it | Bus no. 4 from the main railway station*

ORTO BOTANICO/GIARDINO DEI SEMPLICI (126 A5) (*ØJ G3*)

Small botanical garden laid out in 1545 by Cosimo de' Medici right in the heart of the city. The third-eldest in the world, it now belongs to the University of Florence, as part of the *Museo di Storia Naturale*. Note, in particular, the over 200-year-old oak trees and the yew tree planted in 1720! The collection of various species of carnivorous plant is exciting for the kids. *April–mid-Oct Thu–Tue 10am–7pm, mid-Oct–Mar Sat–Mon 10am–5pm | Admission: 6 euros, reduced: 3 euros | Via Pier Antonio Micheli 3 | www.unifi.it/msn*

INSIDER TIP **VILLA DEMIDOFF** (133 E2)

Run around, have a picnic, go for a walk: all this is possible in the park of the Renaissance villa by Bernardo Buontalenti. *Easter–May and Sept Sat/Sun 10am–6pm, June–Aug until 7pm | Via Fiorentina 282 | Pratolino-Vaglia | Free admission | www.provincia.fi.it/pratolino.htm | Bus no. 25 from the Piazza San Marco/Via La Pira*

FESTIVALS & EVENTS

Whether it's the superb concerts during the Maggio Musicale Fiorentino, the Estate Fiesolana summer festival, the celebration of the iris or the large biennial antiques fair and the wine festivals in the autumn – there is something to suit every taste in Florence. All events under *www.italiafestival.it* or *www.fionline.it/turismo*

FESTIVALS & EVENTS

MARCH/APRIL

25 March (Annunciation Day): ▶ Public festival on the Piazza della SS. Annunziata (123 E1) (*ⓜ G4*)

▶ *Taste:* Culinary fair on a weekend in March; *www.tastefirenze.it*
▶ *Scoppio del Carro* on Easter Sunday: Renaissance firework, during which a historical wooden cart is drawn through the streets, then set on fire between the cathedral and the baptistery (122–123 C–D3) (*ⓜ F4*)

End of April: ▶ Arts and crafts fair ▶ *Mostra Internazionale dell'Artigianato* in the Fortezza da Basso (125 D–E4) (*ⓜ E–F3*); *www.mostraartigianato.it*
▶ *Notte Bianca:* Literally, a 'sleepless night', thanks to the free concerts, performances and other events in the night to 1 May

MAY/JUNE

▶ ★ *Maggio Musicale Fiorentino:* Month-long festival, with operas, concerts and ballets, plus a free closing concert on the Piazza della Signoria (122 C4–5) (*ⓜ D4*); *tickets under Tel. 0 55 21 11 58; www.maggiofiorentino.com*
▶ *Festival Fabbrica Europa:* International festival in the Stazione Leopolda (124 C5) (*ⓜ D3–4*), with dance, music and drama; *www.ffeac.org*
▶ *Mostra dell'Iris:* Huge iris show below the Piazzale Michelangelo (130 B4) (*ⓜ H6*); *www.irisfirenze.it*

Naturally enough, culture plays a huge role in the Florentine calendar, but the city has a raft of other events to show for itself

2nd or 3rd weekend in May: ▶ INSIDER TIP *Artigianato & Palazzo* in the garden of the Palazzo Corsini sul Prato (124–125 C–D5) (*∅ D–E4*), sale of traditional Italian crafts, also made on the premises; *www.artigianatoepalazzo.it*

24 June: ▶ *Calcio in Costume* in honour of the city's patron saint: football with a difference between the four districts in medieval costume on the Piazza Santa Croce (123 E5) (*∅ G5*); in the evening, on the Piazzale Michelangelo (130 B4) (*∅ H6*) large ▶ ● *firework display*, best enjoyed from the other side of the Arno

JULY/AUGUST
▶ *Estate Fiesolana:* One of Italy's oldest festivals, with concerts, ballet and films in the Roman theatre (133 E2); *www.estatefiesolana.it*

▶ *Florence Dance Festival:* Dance festival in July in the inner courtyard of the Museo del Bargello (123 D4) (*∅ G5*), with international programme; *www.florencedance.org*

SEPTEMBER/OCTOBER
7 Sept: ▶ INSIDER TIP *Festa della Rificolona* – Parade featuring innumerable paper lanterns on the Piazza della SS. Annunziata (123 E1) (*∅ G4*) and the Arno

October: ▶ *Festival Internazionale Musica dei Popoli* – Musical culture from many countries at the Auditorium Flog (133 E3); *www.musicadeipopoli.com*

▶ *Biennale Internazionale dell'Antiquariato di Firenze:* Antiques fair at the Palazzo Corsini sull'Arno (122 A4) (*∅ E5*), only in odd-numbered years; *www.biennaleantiquariato.it*

NOVEMBER/DECEMBER
▶ *Festival dei Popoli:* International documentary film festival at the beginning of December; *www.festivaldeipopoli.org*

▶ *Stagione Lirica:* High point of the concert and theatre season. Venues are the main theatres in the city, plus a number of smaller stages; information and tickets under *Tel. 0 55 21 08 04; www.boxol.it*

LINKS, BLOGS, APPS & MORE

LINKS

▶ www.googleartproject.com/museums/uffizi/the-birth-of-venus Not even in the Uffizi can you get so close to these famous works by Giotto, da Vinci, Michelangelo, Titian or Caravaggio. And, what's more, here you can examine them at your leisure

▶ www.firenzeturismo.it The official city portal informs you about current events and museums, helps with the search for accommodation and offers a wide selection of maps and brochures, including city plans or wine guides – to download free of charge

▶ www.italyguides.it/us/florence/florence_italy.htm A virtual journey, with dozens of 360° panorama views, takes you to the most famous spots in the city. Furthermore, you can enjoy these in free HD videos, download audio guides and book cycle tours

▶ www.aboutflorence.com Everything you need to know about your destination at a glance: history, events, virtual tours, current news and offers

BLOGS & FORUMS

▶ www.travelpod.com/travel-blog-city/Italy/Florence/tpod.html Travel portal, with countless community blog entries, pictures and videos describing journeys to Florence

▶ www.lovingflorence.blogspot.com Entertaining blog by a young Florentine woman, who writes about exhibitions, nightlife and scenes of everyday goings-on in the city. The Italian version is also interesting (www.ioamofirenze.blogspot.com), which also includes restaurant tips

▶ blog.luisaviaroma.com Everything you need to know about current fashion trends and events in the city. Online outlet 'Luisa Via Roma' has its finger on the pulse of the fashionistas' world

VIDEOS

▶ www.vimeo.com/18268458 A little romance in your home: take a walk through Florence in the red-gold light of sunset

Regardless of whether you are still preparing your trip or already in Florence: these addresses will provide you with more information, videos and networks to make your holiday even more enjoyable

▶ http://www.youtube.com/watch?v=e xrD5RwjIIo&feature=related If your own computer is a little underpowered: Google has flown with a 3D camera over the city for Google Earth. You can look at the video in various resolutions up to HD quality

▶ www.vimeo.com/8331012 Florence actually stands for summer, sun and warmth. In early 2011, snow brought the city to a standstill, when 30 cm of snow fell in just a few hours. There were too few snow ploughs, traffic ground to a halt and it was eerily silent. A dream of winter, captured on video

▶ Florence Map and Walking Tours Explore the city on foot, turn up some surprises and still know where the next ice cream parlour is. iOS

▶ Florence Giracittš Audioguide App for iOS with more than four hours of audio commentary, 200 images and an interactive map

▶ Uffizi. The Official Guide for iOS through the Uffizi, including detailed information on the most important works of art

▶ http://togo.055055.it Website optimised for smartphones, with details of car parks, petrol stations, traffic jams, cycle paths, wireless LAN hotspots and lots more besides

▶ Michelangelo PhoneClop The right travel look for your Android phone: After each call it shows randomly selected pictures of works by Michelangelo

APPS

▶ www.virtualtourist.com/travel/Europe/Italy/Tuscany/Florence-151105/TravelGuide-Florence.html Travellers offer their comments on restaurants, hotels and sights

▶ www.facebook.com/tfnews?ref=ts The English-language city paper, The Florentine, appears every two weeks; a lively Facebook community has developed from it, too

▶ www.tripwolf.com/en/guide/show/3336/Italy/Florence The Tripwolf community enthusiastically rates and comments on hotels, restaurants and sights in Florence

NETWORKS

TRAVEL TIPS

ARRIVAL

If you are travelling by car, take either the *Brenner highway E 45* (Brenner–Verona–Modena-Bologna), the *Gotthard highway E 35* (Lugano–Milan–Bologna) or the E 43, which runs through Liechtenstein and the San Bernardino tunnel to Milan and then on via Bologna to Florence. Don't leave the highway until the Firenze-Certosa exit; in this way you can avoid the chaos of the suburbs and drive via the Piazzale Michelangelo (well signposted, but take care!) down into the city centre *(centro)*.

Most trains arriving from other major European cities via France, Switzerland (Basel–Milan), Germany or Austria (Munich–Brenner) stop in Florence at the main railway station, S. Maria Novella in the centre; a few go to the through station Firenze Campo di Marte. From here, there is a suburban train to the main station.

RESPONSIBLE TRAVEL

It doesn't take a lot to be environmentally friendly whilst travelling. Don't just think about your carbon footprint whilst flying to and from your holiday destination but also about how you can protect nature and culture abroad. As a tourist it is especially important to respect nature, look out for local products, cycle instead of driving, save water and much more. If you would like to find out more about eco-tourism please visit: *www.ecotourism.org*

The *Aeroporto Amerigo Vespucci* lies just a few kilometres from the city. The airport shuttle *Vola in Bus!* brings you between 5.30am and 11pm to the main railway station. Fare: 5 euros; return ticket: 8 euros. The taxi ride costs you, depending on the time of day, between 20 and 23 euros, plus 1 euro per piece of baggage (except hand luggage). As Florence is actually only classed as a regional airport, there are few direct flights from the European metropolises, e.g. London, Paris or Zurich. The airport at Pisa, the *Aeroporto Galileo Galilei*, is a major North Italian hub with good international links. From here, regular, direct trains take you to the main station in Florence (journey time: 70 mins; price: 5.60 euros).

BANKS

Banks are generally open as follows: *Mon–Fri 8.20am–1.20pm and 2.45pm–3.45pm*. Most branches have ATMs for use with credit cards, too (withdrawals possible up to 250 euros per day).

BICYCLE, SEGWAY & VESPA

Florence by bike hires out various types of two-wheeler. Price example: mountain bike: 4 euros/hr, 21 euros/day; city bike: 3 euros/hr, 14.50 euros/day. A 125-cc scooter costs 45 euros/5 hrs, 68 euros/day *(April–Oct daily 9am–7.30pm, Nov–Mar Mon–Sat 9am–1pm and 3.30pm–7.30pm | Via San Zanobi 120r (125 F5) (𝄞 F3) | Tel. 0 55 48 89 92 | www.florencebybike.it)*.
Segways can be hired from *Segway Firenze* (122 C4) (𝄞 E5) for 18 euros/hr *(mid-Jan–mid-Dec Mon–Sat 9am–1pm*

and 2pm–6pm | Via dei Cimatori 9r | www.segwayfirenze.com).

Florence has the highest number of Vespas in Italy – join the masses and drive a Vespa 125 with a companion for 60 euros/day and 150 euros/weekend, hired from Stradanova (129 D1) (ᴍ D4) (Mar–Sept daily 9am–6pm, Oct–Feb: by appointment only | Via il Prato 50r | Tel. 05 53 98 71 42; mobile 34 97 85 25 32 | www.stradanova.com).

CONSULATES & EMBASSIES

UK CONSULATE
Lungarno Corsini 2 | Tel. 05 52 84 133 | consular.florence@fco.gov.uk

US CONSULATE
Lungarno A. Vespucci, 38 | Tel. 05 52 66 951 | uscitizensflorence@state.gov

CUSTOMS

EU citizens can import and export goods for their personal use tax-free (800 cigarettes, 1 kg tobacco, 90 l of wine, 10 l of spirits over 22 % vol.).

Visitors from other countries, including those travelling to Florence via Switzerland, must observe the following limits, except for items for personal use. Duty free are: max. 50 g perfume, 200 cigarettes, 50 cigars, 250 g tobacco, 1 l of spirits (over 22 % vol.), 2 l of spirits (under 22 % vol.), 2 l of any wine.

DRIVING/CAR HIRE

The entire city centre is only accessible for motor vehicles with prior permission at the following times: Mon–Fri 7.30am–7.30pm and Sat until 6pm, as

BUDGETING

Espresso	1.10 euros	for an espresso, standing in a bar
Carriage	from 50 euros	for a 20-minute ride
Ice cream	from 1.70 euros	for a portion with two flavours
Snack	from 8 euros	for lunch in a bar
Bus ride	1.20 euros	for a ticket valid for 90 mins.
Shoes	from 390 euros	for luxury by Ferragamo

well as June–Sept also Thu–Sat from 11pm–3am (permits available from the Polizia Municipale (Piazza della Calza 2 | (129 D5) (ᴍ D6) | Tel. 0 55 22 10 01 and Piazzale di Porta al Prato 6 | (124 C5) (ᴍ D3) | Tel. 05 53 28 32 84). If you are staying in the centre (Zona ZTL), have your hotel issue you with a permit in advance. It is also forbidden to park in many streets in the outer districts (residents only: divieto di sosta e parcheggio per non residenti). Your car will be towed away and can only be retrieved upon payment of a hefty fine the following day at the Via dell'Arcovata 6 (133 D3) (Tel. 05 57 83 88 82). It makes sense, therefore, to find a safe place to park your car. Parking spaces marked in blue are liable to charge (parking meter); white ones are for residents only!

There are 24-hour car parks at the Porta Romana/Oltrarno (128–129 C–D5) (ᴍ D6–7) (2 euros per hour, 18 euros per day). There are large underground car parks under

the *Parterre* close to the Piazza della Libertà *(entrance in Via Madonna della Tosse | 2 euros/hr, 18 euros/day)*; at the Fortezza da Basso *(entrance in Piazzale Caduti dei Lager | 1.50 euros/hr, 18 euros/day)* (125 D4) (*M E3*) and at the Piazza Beccaria (130 C2) (*M H–J5*) *(1.50 euros/hr, 18 euros/day)*. The underground car parks at the main railway station *(entrance in Via Alamanni)* (125 D6) (*M E4*) and at the Mercato S. Ambrogio *(entrance on Piazza Annigoni)* (130 B2) (*M H5*) cost 1–3 euros/hr, 48–72 euros/day. More information under: *www.firenzeparcheggi.it*
Petrol stations are located on the main arterial roads *(Mon–Fri 7.30am–12.30pm and 3pm (3.30pm)–7.30pm)*. Self-service stations are usually open 24 hours. Lead-free petrol (benzina senza piombo) (95 octane) and diesel (gasolio) are available. It is advisable to book your hire car before you leave home. Almost all major car-hire companies have branches in Florence, e.g. *Avis Autonoleggio (Borgo Ognissanti 128r* (129 D2) (*M E5*) *| Tel. 0 55 21 36 29 | www.avisautonoleggio.it)*. *City Car Rent* also hires out Smarts by the hour at reasonable rates *(Via L. Alamanni 3a* (125 D6) (*M E4*) *| Tel. 05 52 39 92 31 | www.citycarrent.org)*.
Emergency breakdown service (Italy-wide): Automobile Club d'Italia *| Tel. 80 3116*

EMERGENCY

Carabinieri: *Tel. 112*
Fire brigade: *Tel. 115*
Police (accident): *Tel. 113*
Emergency doctor: *Tel. 118*

FIRENZE CARD

If you are staying for a few days, this card really is a worthwhile investment. It is available from hotels, museums or online *(www.firenzecard.it)* and entitles the holder to free admission to 33 museums in the city plus free use of all modes of public transport – both for 72 hours. The card costs 50 euros.

HEALTH

CHEMIST

24-hour opening: *Farmacia Comunale no. 13* at the main railway station (122 A1) (*M E4*); *Farmacia Molteni | Via Calzaiuoli 7r* (122 C4) (*M F5*) and *Farmacia all'Insegna del Moro | Piazza S. Giovanni 20 r* (122 C3) (*M F4*).

HOSPITAL

Outpatient treatment around the clock at the *Pronto Soccorso* at the *Ospedale di Careggi* (133 E2) and at the *Ospedale S. Maria Nuova (Piazza S. Maria Nuova 1* (123 E3) (*M G4*)*)*. For children, go to the *Nuovo Ospedale Meyer (Viale Pieraccini 24, Careggi* (133 E2) *| Tel. 05 55 66 21)*.

INFORMATION IN FLORENCE

Information brochures, city maps and hotel reservations at the tourist offices: *Via Cavour 1r* (122 C2) (*M F4*) *| Mon–Sat 8.30am–6.30pm, Sun 8.30am–1.30pm | Tel. 0 55 29 08 32; Aeroporto Amerigo Vespucci/airport arrivals hall | daily 8.30am–8.30pm | Tel. 0 55 31 58 74; Borgo Santa Croce 29r* (123 E4) (*M G5*) *| Mar–mid-Nov Mon–Sat 9am–7pm, Sun 9am–2pm, mid-Nov–Feb Mon–Sat 9am–5pm, Sun 9am–2pm | Tel. 0 55 23 40 4 44; Piazza Stazione 4* (122 A2) (*M E4*) *| Mon–Sat 8.30am–7pm, Sun 8.30am–2pm | Tel. 0 55 21 22 45.* Written enquiries to: *Via Manzoni 16 | 50121 Firenze | Tel. 05 52 33 20 | www.firenzeturismo.it.*
The tourist offices have free publications, *Informacittà, Firenze dei Teatri* and *Turismo Notizie* which give details of events. *Firenze Spettacolo* (*www.firenzespettacolo.it*) has an overview of the monthly event calendar and is available from

kiosks for 1.80 euros. Every two months, the *Florence Concierge Information (www. florenceconcierge.it)* appears in hotels, as does *Firenze oggi/Florence today*. Another good source of interesting information is *The Florentine*: events, culture, food and drink as well as current news from Florence and the surrounding area (twice a month at hotels, Internet access points, bookshops or language schools; free of charge *(www.theflorentine.net))*.

The website *www.firenzeturismo.it* has tons of information on Florence and Tuscany. Tips for shopping, sightseeing, restaurants, hotels and current exhibitions can be found at *www.firenze.net* and *www.fionline.it*. Take a virtual journey through the city with *www.italyguides. it/us/florence/florence_italy.htm*, while you can access free audio guides and videos at *www.freeaudioguide.com/firenze pro.htm* to get you in the mood for your sightseeing tour.

INTERNET CAFÉS & WIFI

Almost all hotels have wireless LAN connections. Public hot spots are, on the other hand, still relatively thin on the ground. Popular Internet access points are *Internet Train (daily 9am/10am– 8pm/midnight | Via Guelfa 54/56r* (122 C1) *(Ⓜ F4)*; *Via de' Benci 36r* (123 E5) *(Ⓜ G5)*; *Via Porta Rossa 38r* (122 C4) *(Ⓜ F5))*; *Webpuccino (daily 10am–10pm | Via dei Conti 22/r* (125 F5) *(Ⓜ F4)*.

At the *Martelli bookshop* you can sip on a latte macchiato and surf at the same time *(Easy Internet | Mon–Sat 9am–8pm, Sun 10am–8pm | Via Martelli 22* (122 C2) *(Ⓜ F4) | www.easyinternetcafe.it)*.

INVOICES & RECEIPTS

According to Italian law, all invoices and receipts – even the ones for a quick *caffè* in a bar – must be retained until the customer is at least 100m (110yd) away from the place of purchase. The Guardia di Finanzia (literally the 'tax police') carry out frequent spot-checks to counter possible tax evasion by shopkeepers and restaurant proprietors.

PHONE & MOBILE PHONE

Buy a telephone card *(scheda telefonica)* at tobacconist's and kiosks to use a public telephone. Remember to tear off the corner at the perforation before using! For calls abroad to landline phones, it's best to use a *scheda telefonica internazionale*,

CURRENCY CONVERTER

£	€	€	£
1	1.10	1	0.90
3	3.30	3	2.70
5	5.50	5	4.50
13	14.30	13	11.70
40	44	40	36
75	82.50	75	67.50
120	132	120	108
250	275	250	225
500	550	500	450

$	€	€	$
1	0.70	1	1.40
3	2.10	3	4.20
5	3.50	5	7
13	9.10	13	18.20
40	28	40	56
75	52.50	75	105
120	84	120	168
250	175	250	350
500	350	500	700

For current exchange rates see www.xe.com

which is cheaper than a standard one. Find out about the cheapest network when you get to Florence and program your mobile accordingly. The area code in Italy is part of the telephone number and must always be dialled (including the zero!). The international dialling code for Italy is 0039. Dial 0044 for calls from Italy to the UK; 001 to the USA; reverse-charge calls under *Tel. 8 00 17 24 90.*

POST

In all EU countries except Italy postage for standard letters and postcards is 75 cents. Stamps can be bought at Post Of-fices *(Posta Centrale | Mon–Fri 8.15am–7pm, Sat 8.15am–12.30pm | Via Pelliceria 1 (122 C4) (∅ F5))* and in many tobac-conist's (look out for signs with a white 'T' on a black background).

PRE-TRAVEL INFORMATION

ITALIAN STATE TOURIST BOARD
– 1 Princes Street, London W1B 2AY | Tel. 020 74 08 12 54 | info.london@enit.it
– 630 Fifth Avenue - Suite 1565, New York 10111 | Tel. 212 245-5618 | newyork@enit.it
– PO Box Q802 - QVB NSW 1230, Level 4, 46 Market Street, Sydney, NSW 2000, Aus-tralia | Tel. 02 9262 1666 | sydney@enit.it

PUBLIC TRANSPORT

Transport company ATAF's tickets can be purchased in bars, tobacconist's or kiosks and must be validated on board the bus. Between 9pm and 6am, you can buy tickets for 2 euros from the bus driver. Be careful, though: Try to have the correct amount with you, as the driver is not obliged to have sufficient change! Fare dodging is penalised with a fine of at least 40 euros! Children up to 1m (1.10yd) in height travel free. A ticket valid for 90 mins *(biglietto sem-plice)* costs 1.20 euros; a ticket for four journeys *(quattro corse)* 4.70 euros; a 24-hour *biglietto 24 ore* 5 euros and a 3-day ticket *(biglietto tre giorni)* 12 euros. Timetable information is available in the entrance hall of the main railway sta-tion *(daily 7.30am–7.30pm)* and online at *www.ataf.net.*

In 2010, the first route of the new tram system, the *tramvia,* was opened. It links the suburb of Scandicci in the southwest with the main railway station.

SIGHTSEEING TOURS

Caf Tour&Travel offers tours of Florence and trips into the surrounding country-side. Starting point is the Piazza dell'Unità (122 B2) (∅ E–F4) *(Nov–Mar 11am, April–Oct also 4pm | Ticket: 20 euros; children: 10 euros | Tel. 0 55 21 06 12 | www.caftours. com). Florence Open Tour* has a route which takes you all over town in two hours. The trip is touted as a 'hop on – hop off' model: You can use your ticket for 24 hours for as many journeys as you like, getting on and off the bus whenever it takes your fancy *(Nov–Feb 9.30am–5pm, Mar–May and Oct daily 9am–9pm, June–Sept 9am–11pm | 20 euros; reduced: 10 euros | www.florenceopentour.it).*

A tour with the ● *electric minibus C3* al-most constitutes a city sightseeing tour in itself. It passes along the narrow streets of the old town centre and takes you across to the other side of the Arno. And, what's more, the journey won't break the bank *(1.20 euros).*

It is essential to book in advance if you want to take advantage of the wide range of individual sightseeing tours through the city on foot or by bike which are offered by various agencies, for exam-ple, *Flora Promo Tuscany (Tel. 05 52 10 31 | www.florapromotuscany.com), Art Viva*

Walking Tours (Tel. 05 52 64 50 33 | www. italy.artviva.com) and I bike Florence (Tel. 05 50 12 39 94 | www.ibikeflorence.com).

SMOKING

Smoking is strictly prohibited in all public buildings, restaurants, bars, discos etc., except where a separate smoking area has been designated. Believe it or not, the Italians respect the ban – otherwise the fines are steep: between 275 and 2200 euros!

TAXI

In Florence it is virtually impossible to flag down a taxi in the street. Either you call a radio taxi *(Tel. 0 55 43 90; 0 55 47 98; 0 55 42 42)*, or go to one of the taxi ranks: *Main railway station* (122 A1–2) *(𝄚 E4)*, *Parterre* (126 B3) *(𝄚 G2)*, *Piazza della Libertà* (126 A4) *(𝄚 G2)*, *Piazza della Repubblica* (122 C3–4) *(𝄚 F5)*, *Piazza San Marco* (126 A5) *(𝄚 G4)*, *Piazza Santa Maria Novella* (122 A2–3) *(𝄚 E4)*, *Piazza Santa Trìnita* (122 B4) *(𝄚 E5)*, *Piazza Ferrucci* (130 C4) *(𝄚 J6)* and *Porta Romana* (128–139 C–D5) *(𝄚 D7)*. The minimum fare if you take a taxi at a taxi rank is 3.30 euros; if you book by phone, 5.30 euros. A supplement is charged after 10pm, on Sundays and public holidays and for each piece of baggage carried in the boot of the car. Women travelling alone at night (9pm–2am) receive a 10 per cent discount (ask for the *sconto*!).

THEFT

Thefts of identity cards, passports and vehicles, etc. must be reported to the police immediately, at a district police station or the headquarters *(Borgo Ognissanti 48 |* (129 D2) *(𝄚 E5) | Tel. 05 52 48 11)*.

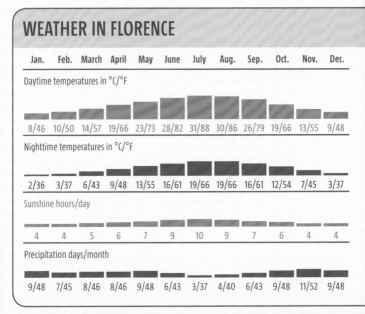

WEATHER IN FLORENCE

	Jan.	Feb.	March	April	May	June	July	Aug.	Sep.	Oct.	Nov.	Dec.
Daytime temperatures in °C/°F												
	8/46	10/50	14/57	19/66	23/73	28/82	31/88	30/86	26/79	19/66	13/55	9/48
Nighttime temperatures in °C/°F												
	2/36	3/37	6/43	9/48	13/55	16/61	19/66	19/66	16/61	12/54	7/45	3/37
Sunshine hours/day												
	4	4	5	6	7	9	10	9	7	6	4	4
Precipitation days/month												
	9/48	7/45	8/46	8/46	9/48	6/43	3/37	4/40	6/43	9/48	11/52	9/48

USEFUL PHRASES ITALIAN

PRONUNCIATION

c, cc	before e or i like ch in "church", e.g. ciabatta, otherwise like k
ch, cch	like k, e.g. pacchi, che
g, gg	before e or i like j in "just", e.g. gente, otherwise like g in "get"
gl	like "lli" in "million", e.g. figlio
gn	as in "cognac", e.g. bagno
sc	before e or i like sh, e.g. uscita
sch	like sk in "skill", e.g. Ischia
z	at the beginning of a word like dz in "adze", otherwise like ts

An accent on an Italian word shows that the stress is on the last syllable.
In other cases we have shown which syllable is stressed by placing a dot below
the relevant vowel.

IN BRIEF

Yes/No/Maybe	Sì/No/Forse
Please/Thank you	Per favore/Grazie
Excuse me, please!	Scusa!/Mi scusi
May I ...?/Pardon?	Posso ...? / Come dice?/Prego?
I would like to .../Have you got ...?	Vorrei .../Avete ...?
How much is ...?	Quanto costa ...?
I (don't) like that	(Non) mi piace
good/bad	buono/cattivo/bene/male
broken/doesn't work	guasto/non funziona
too much/much/little/all/nothing	troppo/molto/poco/tutto/niente
Help!/Attention!/Caution!	aiuto!/attenzione!/prudenza!
ambulance/police/fire brigade	ambulanza/polizia/vigili del fuoco
Prohibition/forbidden/danger/dangerous	divieto/vietato/pericolo/pericoloso
May I take a photo here/of you?	Posso fotografar La?

GREETINGS, FAREWELL

Good morning!/afternoon!/ evening!/night!	Buon giorno!/Buon giorno!/ Buona sera!/Buona notte!
Hello! / Goodbye!/See you	Ciao!/Salve! / Arrivederci!/Ciao!
My name is ...	Mi chiamo ...
What's your name?	Come si chiama?/Come ti chiami
I'm from ...	Vengo da ...

Parli italiano?

"Do you speak Italian?" This guide will help you to say the basic words and phrases in Italian.

DATE & TIME

Monday/Tuesday/Wednesday	lunedì/martedì/mercoledì
Thursday/Friday/Saturday	giovedì/venerdì/sabato
Sunday/holiday/ working day	domenica/(giorno) festivo/ (giorno) feriale
today/tomorrow/yesterday	oggi/domani/ieri
hour/minute	ora/minuto
day/night/week/month/year	giorno/notte/settimana/mese/anno
What time is it?	Che ora è? Che ore sono?
It's three o'clock/It's half past three	Sono le tre/Sono le tre e mezza
a quarter to four	le quattro meno un quarto/ un quarto alle quattro

TRAVEL

open/closed	aperto/chiuso
entrance/exit	entrata/uscita
departure/arrival	partenza/arrivo
toilets/ladies/gentlemen	bagno/toilette/signore/signori
(no) drinking water	acqua (non) potabile
Where is ...?/Where are ...?	Dov'è ...?/Dove sono ...?
left/right/straight ahead/back	sinistra/destra/dritto/indietro
close/far	vicino/lontano
bus/tram	bus/tram
taxi/cab	taxi/tassì
bus stop/cab stand	fermata/posteggio taxi
parking lot/parking garage	parcheggio/parcheggio coperto
street map/map	pianta/mappa
train station/harbour	stazione/porto
airport	aeroporto
schedule/ticket	orario/biglietto
supplement	supplemento
single/return	solo andata/andata e ritorno
train/track	treno/binario
platform	banchina/binario
I would like to rent ...	Vorrei noleggiare ...
a car/a bicycle	una macchina/una bicicletta
a boat	una barca
petrol/gas station	distributore/stazione di servizio
petrol/gas / diesel	benzina/diesel/gasolio
breakdown/repair shop	guasto/officina

FOOD & DRINK

Could you please book a table for tonight for four?	Vorrei prenotare per stasera un tavolo per quattro?
on the terrace/by the window	sulla terrazza/ vicino alla finestra
The menu, please/	La carta/il menù, per favore
Could I please have ...?	Potrei avere ...?
bottle/carafe/glass	bottiglia/caraffa/bicchiere
knife/fork/spoon/salt/pepper	coltello/forchetta/cucchiaio/sale/pepe
sugar/vinegar/oil/milk/cream/lemon	zucchero/aceto/olio/latte/panna/limone
cold/too salty/not cooked	freddo/troppo salato/non cotto
with/without ice/sparkling	con/senza ghiaccio/gas
vegetarian/allergy	vegetariano/vegetariana/allergia
May I have the bill, please?	Vorrei pagare/Il conto, per favore
bill/tip	conto/mancia

SHOPPING

Where can I find...?	Dove posso trovare ...?
I'd like .../I'm looking for ...	Vorrei .../Cerco ...
Do you put photos onto CD?	Vorrei masterizzare delle foto su CD?
pharmacy/shopping centre/kiosk	farmacia/centro commerciale/edicola
department store/supermarket	grandemagazzino/supermercato
baker/market/grocery	forno/ mercato/negozio alimentare
photographic items/newspaper shop/	articoli per foto/giornalaio
100 grammes/1 kilo	un etto/un chilo
expensive/cheap/price/more/less	caro/economico/prezzo/di più/di meno
organically grown	di agricoltura biologica

ACCOMMODATION

I have booked a room	Ho prenotato una camera
Do you have any ... left?	Avete ancora ...
single room/double room	una (camera) singola/doppia
breakfast/half board/	prima colazione/mezza pensione/
full board (American plan)	pensione completa
at the front/seafront/lakefront	con vista/con vista sul mare/lago
shower/sit-down bath/balcony/terrace	doccia/bagno/balcone/terrazza
key/room card	chiave/scheda magnetica
luggage/suitcase/bag	bagaglio/valigia/borsa

BANKS, MONEY & CREDIT CARDS

bank/ATM/pin code	banca/bancomat/ codice segreto
cash/credit card	in contanti/carta di credito
bill/coin/change	banconota/moneta/il resto

HEALTH

doctor/dentist/paediatrician	medico/dentista/pediatra
hospital/emergency clinic	ospedale/pronto soccorso/guardia medica
fever/pain/inflamed/injured	febbre/dolori/infiammato/ferito
diarrhoea/nausea/sunburn	diarrea/nausea/scottatura solare
plaster/bandage/ointment/cream	cerotto/fasciatura/pomata/crema
pain reliever/tablet/suppository	antidolorifico/compressa/supposta

POST, TELECOMMUNICATIONS & MEDIA

stamp/letter/postcard	francobollo/lettera/cartolina
I need a landline phone card/ I'm looking for a prepaid card for my mobile	Mi serve una scheda telefonica per la rete fissa/Cerco una scheda prepagata per il mio cellulare
Where can I find internet access?	Dove trovo un accesso internet?
dial/connection/engaged	comporre/linea/occupato
socket/adapter/charger	presa/riduttore/caricabatterie
computer/battery/rechargeable battery	computer/batteria/accumulatore
internet address (URL)/e-mail address	indirizzo internet/indirizzo email
internet connection/wifi	collegamento internet/wi-fi
e-mail/file/print	email/file/stampare

LEISURE, SPORTS & BEACH

beach/bathing beach	spiaggia/bagno/stabilimento balneare
sunshade/lounger/cable car/chair lift	ombrellone/sdraio/funivia/seggiovia
(rescue) hut/avalanche	rifugio/valanga

NUMBERS

0	zero	15	quindici
1	uno	16	sedici
2	due	17	diciassette
3	tre	18	diciotto
4	quattro	19	diciannove
5	cinque	20	venti
6	sei	21	ventuno
7	sette	50	cinquanta
8	otto	100	cento
9	nove	200	duecento
10	dieci	1000	mille
11	undici	2000	duemila
12	dodici	10000	diecimila
13	tredici	½	un mezzo
14	quattordici	¼	un quarto

NOTES

FOR YOUR NEXT HOLIDAY ...

MARCO POLO TRAVEL GUIDES

MARCO ⊕ POLO
With ROAD ATLAS & PULL-OUT MAP
LAKE GARDA
...E BALDO WITH MOUNTAIN BIKE
...in Malcesine takes bikes too
...GES " IN SALÒ
...date "bacetti"
Insider Tips

MARCO ⊕ POLO
With STREET ATLAS & PULL-OUT MAP
NEW YORK
...NOWS, WILD FLOWERS AND SKYSCRAPERS
...o chic: the High Line in Chelsea
...AIL ON CLOUD NINE
...Top bar at 230 Fifth Street
Insider Tips

MARCO ⊕ POLO
With ROAD ATLAS & PULL-OUT MAP
FRENCH RIVIERA
NICE, CANNES & MONACO
SPECTACULAR GRAND CANYON DU VERDON
Breath-taking scenery that takes some beating
SNIFFING THE AIR
The perfume manufacturers of Grasse
Insider Tips
www.marcopolouk.com

MARCO ⊕ POLO
With STREET ATLAS & PULL-OUT MAP
BERLIN
A STUNNING ISLAND JUST FOR ART
Showcasing treasures from around the world
STAY COOL AT NIGHT
...scene sets the trend
Insider Tips
www.marcopolouk.com

MARCO ⊕ POLO
With ROAD ATLAS & PULL-OUT MAP
MALLORCA
...AN FLAIR IN THE MEDITERRANEAN
...Mallorca's most beautiful beach
..." CROWD MEET
...enda in Deià
Insider Tips

- PACKED WITH INSIDER TIPS
- BEST WALKS AND TOURS
- FULL-COLOUR PULL-OUT MAP
  AND STREET ATLAS

STREET ATLAS

The green line ▬▬ indicates the Walking tours (p. 96–101)

All tours are also marked on the pull-out map

Exploring Florence

The map on the back cover shows how the area has been sub-divided

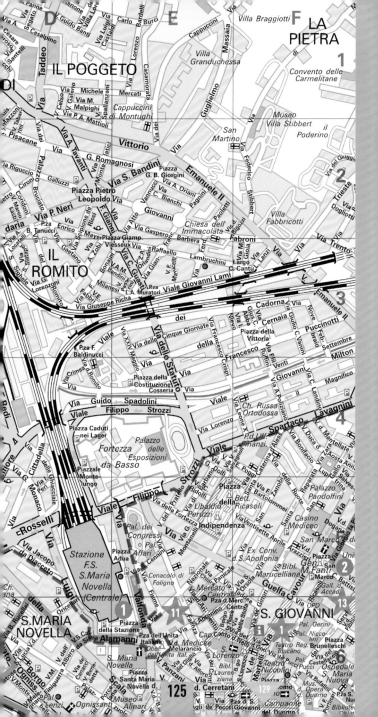

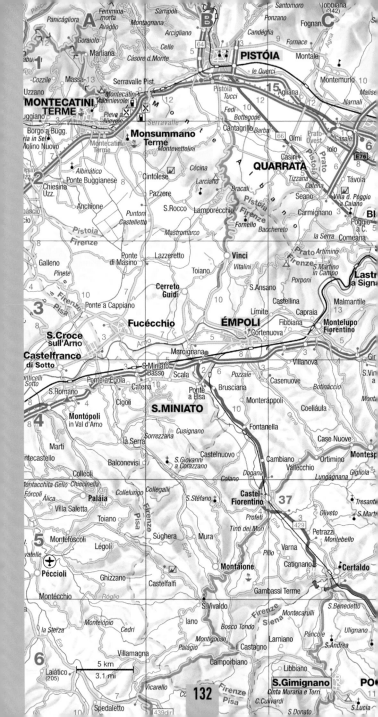

This index lists a selection of the streets and squares shown in the Street Atlas

KEY TO STREET ATLAS

German			English / French / Italian
Autobahn Motorway (Freeway)			Autoroute Autostrada
Vierspurige Straße Road with four lanes			Route à quatre voies Strada a quattro corsie
Bundes- / Fernstraße Federal / trunk road			Route fédérale / nationale Strada statale / di grande comunicazione
Hauptstraße Main road			Route principale Strada principale
Fußgängerzone - Einbahnstraße Pedestrian zone - One way road			Zone piétonne - Rue à sens unique Zona pedonale - Via a senso unico
Eisenbahn mit Bahnhof Railway with station			Chemin de fer avec gare Ferrovia con stazione
U-Bahn Underground (railway)			Métro Metropolitana
Buslinie - Straßenbahn Bus-route - Tramway			Ligne d'autocar - Tram Linea d'autobus - Tram
Information - Jugendherberge Information - Youth hostel			Information - Auberge de jeunesse Informazioni - Ostello della gioventù
Kirche - Sehenswerte Kirche Church - Church of interest			Église - Église remarquable Chiesa - Chiesa di notevole interesse
Synagoge - Moschee Synagogue - Mosque			Synagogue - Mosquée Sinagoga - Moschea
Polizeistation - Postamt Police station - Post office			Poste de police - Bureau de poste Posto di polizia - Ufficio postale
Krankenhaus Hospital			Hôpital Ospedale
Denkmal - Funk- oder Fernsehturm Monument - Radio or TV tower			Monument - Tour d'antennes Monumento - Pilone radio o TV
Theater - Taxistand Theatre - Taxi rank			Théâtre - Station taxi Teatro - Posteggio di tassì
Feuerwache - Schule Fire station - School			Poste de pompiers - École Guardia del fuoco - Scuola
Freibad - Hallenbad Open air - / Indoor swimming pool			Piscine en plein air - Piscine couverte Piscina all'aperto - Piscina coperta
Öffentliche Toilette - Ausflugslokal Public toilet - Restaurant			Toilette publique - Restaurant Gabinetto pubblico - Ristorante
Parkhaus - Parkplatz Indoor car park - Car park			Parking couvert - Parking Autosilo - Area di parcheggio
Stadtspaziergänge Walking tours			Promenades en ville Passeggiate urbane
MARCO POLO Highlight			MARCO POLO Highlight

INDEX

This index lists all sights and destinations plus a number of important streets and squares featured in this guide. Numbers in bold indicate a main entry.